CONTENTS

PART FIVE
BACKGROUND

PART ONE

INTRODUCTION

HOW TO STUDY A PLAY

Studying on your own requires self-discipline and a carefully thought-out work plan in order to be effective.

- Drama is a special kind of writing (the technical term is 'genre') because it needs a performance in the theatre to arrive at a full interpretation of its meaning. Try to imagine that you are a member of the audience when reading the play. Think about how it could be presented on the stage, not just about the words on the page.

- Drama is always about conflict of some sort (which may be below the surface). Identify the conflicts in the play and you will be close to identifying the large ideas or themes which bind all the parts together.

- Make careful notes on themes, character, plot and any sub-plots of the play.

- Why do you like or dislike the characters in the play? How do your feelings towards them develop and change?

- Playwrights find non-realistic ways of allowing an audience to see into the minds and motives of their characters, for example, aside or music. Consider how such dramatic devices are used in the play you are studying.

- Think of the playwright writing the play. Why were these particular arrangements of events, characters and speeches chosen?

- Cite exact sources for all quotations, whether from the text itself or from critical commentaries. Wherever possible find your own examples from the play to back up your opinions.

- Where appropriate, comment in detail on the language of the passage you have quoted.

- Always express your ideas in your own words.

These York Notes offer an introduction to *Othello* and cannot substitute for close reading of the text and the study of secondary sources.

 CHECK THE NET

A site well worth visiting and with useful and accessible short sections on historical and social contexts, and a reading list, is **www.bardweb.net**.

READING *OTHELLO*

Othello is one of Shakespeare's most popular plays. It has had a long and successful stage history and was one of the first plays to be performed after the theatres were reopened in 1660. Since then a number of great actors and actresses have taken on the principal roles. *Othello* has never gone in and out of fashion in the way that some of Shakespeare's other plays have. This is possibly because of its universal theme – love – and its rather narrow focus on three characters' lives and concerns, which are minutely observed for a short space of time; the play exerts what Norman Sanders has called a 'relentless emotional grip' on its audience. We are asked to observe an essentially private tragedy in *Othello*: the destruction of a noble man and his marriage. The contrasting emotions that the central situation evokes – passion, hatred, envy, jealousy – resonate in any age. Many critics have noted the psychological complexity and depth with which Shakespeare examines these powerful feelings. The intensity of the drama is heightened because all the subsidiary characters and events are designed to throw light on the protagonists and their actions. The play is intriguing because of the contradictions and tensions it contains; a black mercenary marries a white aristocrat, an evil ensign corrupts a great soldier, over-powering love is turned to overwhelming jealousy. The events of the play unfold in two very different locations, Venice and Cyprus, which mirror the oppositions within the characters: civilisation is pitted against a dangerous outpost which is threatened by a heathen nation.

In *Othello* Shakespeare incorporates a number of features of the drama of his age, while also departing from tradition. The traditional elements include revenge, which enables the dramatist to explore the themes of violence and justice, and the introduction of a **Machiavellian** villain, who is a complex and fascinating study in evil. Through his characterisation of Iago Shakespeare introduces the theme of appearance and reality, which is almost an obsession in Jacobean drama. Othello is in many ways a traditional tragic hero. Many would argue that he is brought down by **hubris**, a kind of blind pride which afflicts a number of Elizabethan and Jacobean

CONTEXT

There are a number of Moorish characters in Elizabethan and Jacobean drama. The Moor Aaron, in Shakespeare's early play, *Titus Andronicus* (1583), is a stereotypical villain – a cunning, ruthless and lecherous figure. Othello's characterisation as a noble and heroic figure is a dramatic departure from the usual seventeenth-century depiction of Moors.

protagonists. But Othello is also unique in the literature of the time: he was the first black hero to be presented on the stage. Shakespeare's portrayal of a noble Moor, xenophobia and racial stereotypes make the play as relevant today as it was in the seventeenth century. Many feel that this Shakespearean hero is one of the greatest lovers ever created by a writer; there is certainly something truly grand about Othello and the passions he is swayed by. We might feel that the portrayal of women, their troublesome sexuality and male–female relationships make the play compelling for a modern audience. The female stereotypes which the male characters force on their women – chaste, silent and obedient wife and assertive whore – are still the subject of heated debate. The play also exerts a hold on our emotions because of Shakespeare's extensive use of **dramatic irony**. *Othello* is full of ironic contradictions which absorb and worry us. We are never allowed to relax while we watch this play because our attention is focused either on the source of so much of the **irony**, Iago, or the hapless victims of his ironic words and actions.

When you read and study *Othello* it is important to remember that you are dealing with a piece of literature that was written specifically for the theatre. There are inconsistencies in the plot and time scheme, but they disappear when the play is performed because an audience does not have time to pay them much attention. (For a discussion of the time scheme in *Othello* see **Language and structure**.) Try to imagine the different ways in which lines can be delivered and how this might affect your understanding of characters and events; there can be no one 'correct' Othello, Desdemona or Iago, since actors and directors bring their own ideas and emphases to the text. Your interpretation of the text will be coloured by your own responses to and experiences of the central themes. It is worth considering the ways in which other readers have responded to *Othello* too. Until relatively recently the question of Othello's race has frequently been ignored or dealt with perfunctorily; critics have preferred to concentrate on the exact nature of the hero's nobility (or lack of it) and the villain's devilment. For a full discussion of the contradictory readings of Othello, Iago and the themes of the play see **Critical approaches and Critical history**.

CONTEXT

In Shakespeare's day, the term 'Moor' was used to describe Africans from a variety of regions, so we cannot be sure of Othello's exact racial origins.

PART TWO

THE TEXT

NOTE ON THE TEXT

 **CHECK THE BOOK**

For a history of *Othello* in performance from 1660–1980s, see Virginia Mason Vaughan, *Othello: A Contextual History*.

It is not possible to date the composition of *Othello* exactly, but recent editors suggest that the play was probably written between September 1603 and the summer of the following year. There was a performance at the Banqueting House at Whitehall in London on 1 November 1604 attended by James I. Thereafter *Othello* was performed relatively frequently – in and outside the capital – during the early part of the seventeenth century; a testament to its popularity with audiences, which has not waned in succeeding centuries.

The first published version of *Othello* – the Quarto – appeared in 1622. This late Quarto is thought to have been based on transcripts from Shakespeare's own papers. In the following year *Othello* was included in the Folio, the first collection of Shakespeare's plays to be printed. The Quarto and Folio editions of the text differ somewhat. The Folio is 160 lines longer and in this text oaths are cut (possibly to pacify censors), Desdemona's 'willow song' is added and Emilia's role is extended in the last scenes of the play. Both texts are considered defective, although most modern editors agree that the Folio includes revisions that Shakespeare made after the first public performances of *Othello*. As a result, most modern editions of the play are based on the Folio text. The text used in the preparation of these Notes is the Arden Shakespeare edition, edited by E. A. J. Honigmann (see **Further reading** for details).

As with all his other plays Shakespeare went to sources for inspiration, transforming them for his own dramatic purposes. His conception of an heroic black Moor as tragic protagonist was original and unusual. At this time there were various stereotypes of the black man, most of them negative. From the medieval period onwards the devil was often depicted in art as a black man surrounded by the flames of hell. Other traditions associated the black man with lust, sin and death. Prior to Othello, blackamoors in plays and pageants were usually sinister figures (Shakespeare's other Moorish character, Aaron in *Titus Andronicus,* is a villain). In *Othello* Shakespeare explores and subverts these stereotypes.

The plot of *Othello* is taken from a collection of tales by the Italian writer Giambattisa Cinzio Giraldi – the *Hecatommithi* (1565), which was also used as a source for *Measure for Measure.* It is not certain whether Shakespeare used the Italian original or a French translation by Gabriel Chappuys, which appeared in 1584. Stanley, Wells and Gary Taylor, the editors of the recent *Complete Works* suggest that there are verbal echoes of both texts in *Othello.* In Cinzio's novella the Moor and his wife (Disdemona) live contentedly together in Venice for some time before the Ensign (who falls in love with the Moor's wife) persuades him that his spouse has been unfaithful with Cassio, a captain. Together the Moor and his ensign plan to kill Disdemona. The Ensign commits the murder, bludgeoning Disdemona to death with a stocking filled with sand. The ceiling is then collapsed on the body to make the death look like an accident. The Moor denies his part in the murder and is sent into exile, where he is killed by Disdemona's kinsmen. The Ensign continues his life of crime, eventually dying as a result of the torture inflicted on him during a period of imprisonment he endures for committing another felony.

Shakespeare clearly stuck to Cinzio's tale closely, although there are significant differences between this story and *Othello.* Shakespeare compresses the timescale to heighten the emotional impact of events and makes use of two contrasting locations. He introduces the characters of Roderigo and Brabantio (Desdemona's father) and the war between the Turks and Venetians. Roderigo's presence enables us to observe the workings of the villain Iago's mind more closely, while Brabantio, and his death from grief, help us to view Othello's marriage from another perspective. The war – between infidels and Christians – helps establish the atmosphere of tension and opposition, which compliments the events that occur within Othello's marriage. The political battle also mirrors the battle that we see within Othello, who was born an infidel but has adopted the Christian religion of the state he serves. The lust of the ensign in the novella is replaced by the personal and professional jealousy of

CHECK THE NET

For extracts from sources and links to other sites that include for example *Hecatommithi* see **www.Shakespeare -online.com/ sources**.

Iago, providing thematic continuity. Interestingly, Shakespeare makes Emilia an unwitting aid to her husband. In Cinzio's tale the Ensign's wife is fully aware of her husband's villainous practices but is too frightened to speak out. It seems that Shakespeare wants to make Iago independent in his malignity: in *Othello* the villain is a lone figure who relies on no one.

Shakespeare possibly went to other sources too. Norman Sanders has suggested that the military sections of *Othello* might have been influenced by a tale in Barnabe Rich's *Farewell to Military Profession* (1581), which Shakespeare had used when writing *Twelfth Night* in 1600–1. Details of Othello's military and personal life might have been taken from Plutarch's *Life of Cato Unican* and the preface of Leo's the *History and Description of Africa* by John Parry, which was published in 1600. Kenneth Muir has suggested a number of other possible sources that might have provided Shakespeare with details that he could have used to construct Othello's history, including Pliny's *Natural History*. Muir also suggests that Shakespeare made use of Sir Lewes Lewkenor's translation of Cardinal Contareno's *The Commonwealth and Government of Venice* (1599) to obtain information about The Venetian state.

Synopsis

The Moor Othello, a valiant and respected general has fallen in love with and secretly married a wealthy Venetian aristocrat, Desdemona. When her father, Brabantio is informed of this (on the night of the marriage) he angrily goes in search of Othello and then makes his way to the senate to protest. At the same time the Venetian council have been seeking Othello; they wish to send him on an urgent military mission to defend Cyprus from a Turkish invasion. Othello is dispatched immediately, having defended his actions successfully.

Othello's embittered and cynical ensign (standard-bearer), Iago, accompanies Othello and Desdemona to Cyprus. He is angry because he has not received a promotion that he believes was due to him. A young Florentine soldier, Cassio, has been made lieutenant over him. Iago seeks to revenge himself – for personal and professional reasons – on both Cassio and Othello. Iago has already made trouble for Othello (he informed Brabantio of the elopement, with the assistance of Roderigo, a disappointed suitor for Desdemona's hand): now he plans a more subtle and vicious revenge. He goads Roderigo into challenging Cassio, whom he has plied with drink. A fight ensues. Cassio is disgraced and dismissed from his post. Iago then persuades Othello that Desdemona is in love with Cassio and has committed adultery with him. He contrives ocular proof of this, making use of a handkerchief belonging to Desdemona, which is supposedly found in Cassio's bedchamber (Desdemona has in fact dropped this handkerchief; it was picked up and passed on to Iago by Emilia, who is Iago's wife and Desdemona's lady-in-waiting). Although reluctant to believe his wife unchaste, Othello becomes convinced that Desdemona is a whore and is seized by jealousy. His pride and faith in love are shattered and he seeks revenge on Desdemona and Cassio.

Othello asks Iago to kill Cassio. Iago again persuades Roderigo to assist him but this attack does not go as planned. Iago stabs and kills Roderigo after a bungled attempt on Cassio's life. Meanwhile, Othello has smothered Desdemona in her bed. Emilia comes to inform Othello of the attack on Cassio and finds her mistress dead. She calls out for help. Iago's plots are gradually revealed, largely by his wife, who is killed by her husband for speaking the truth, and Othello realises his own great and terrible folly. Full of remorse the Moor kills himself, thereby regaining some of the nobility that he has lost during his descent into jealousy. Iago is led away for torture.

> **CONTEXT**
>
> The Moors, Islamic inhabitants of Northern Africa, conquered Spain in the eighth century. From the eleventh to fifteenth centuries, Christians reconquered Spain, and many Moors adopted a more European culture. Some became Christians.

ACT I

CHECK THE FILM

In the 1952 Orson Welles production, the film opens with Desdemona and Othello's funeral procession. Iago is seen suspended in a cage, his eyes glinting wickedly. This opening clearly suggests the inevitability of the events that occur. Do you believe this opening is true to Shakespeare's intentions for *Othello*?

- Roderigo is unhappy with Iago for failing to promote his marriage to Desdemona.
- Iago and Roderigo inform Brabantio that his daughter, Desdemona, has secretly married the general Othello.

The opening scene takes place in a street in Venice at night. Iago and Roderigo enter, deep in conversation. Roderigo is displeased with Iago; we discover that he feels he has been cheated because a young Venetian aristocrat, Desdemona, has married Othello the Moor without her father's knowledge. Roderigo has paid Iago to promote a marriage between himself and Desdemona. He feels Iago has not worked hard enough on his behalf and is indignant that his money has been wasted. Iago attempts to restore Roderigo's faith in him by describing how much he hates Othello. We learn that Iago has been passed over for promotion. Instead, Othello, a general, has made Michael Cassio his lieutenant (second in command). Iago holds Cassio in contempt and is bitter about his own fortunes (he is Othello's 'ancient', his ensign, line 32). He says that he only feigns loyalty to Othello; he is determined to revenge himself on the Moor for ignoring his experience and competence in favour of a man who, he says, has little practical experience of soldiering.

Iago urges Roderigo to rouse Brabantio (Desdemona's father) from his bed and inform him of the marriage. Brabantio appears at his window, annoyed at being disturbed. He recognises Roderigo and castigates him for lurking outside his house; he has already told Roderigo that he is not an acceptable match for Desdemona and imagines that he has come wooing again. At first Brabantio does not believe the tale that Roderigo and Iago tell, but he is gradually persuaded to accept that his daughter has eloped when Roderigo politely asks him to see whether Desdemona is asleep in her room.

Iago takes the opportunity to leave. He tells Roderigo that he must return to Othello, who can be found at the Sagittary. The unhappy Brabantio reappears. Having accepted Roderigo and Iago's version of events, he now wants to locate his daughter and the Moor. Roderigo leads the way.

COMMENTARY

The play opens with two characters engaged in a dispute; from the very start of *Othello* the scene is set for conflict. A mood of confusion and intrigue is established too. The audience does not know what the characters are talking about to begin with because the subject of so much of their conversation (Othello) is never referred to by name. However, we quickly understand that Iago and Roderigo dislike the Moor. Roderigo refers to him as 'the thicklips' (line 65), while Iago paints an unflattering portrait of the general, who is described as proud, pompous and boastful. Iago's contempt for Cassio indicates that he feels Othello's judgement is faulty too. We swiftly realise that Iago is a bitter and disappointed man. Should we trust what he says of others? Iago stresses that he only follows Othello to 'serve my turn upon him' (line 41) and is 'not what I am' (line 64). In short, Iago openly admits that he is a self-serving deceiver. His willingness to take money from Roderigo to promote a match with Desdemona also looks mercenary, especially when we learn that Brabantio has a dim view of Roderigo.

Iago is a cynical malcontent. He despises men who wear their hearts on their sleeves and other 'honest knaves' (line 48) who fail to look after their own interests. He admires men who can exploit their masters and line their own pockets by pretending to be honest and trustworthy. His energetic speeches are full of egotistical disgust and indignation. When he suggests rousing Brabantio we learn that Iago also delights in making trouble. Roderigo speaks to the senator politely, but it is Iago's crude descriptions of Othello 'tupping your white ewe' (line 88) which strike home. The animal imagery Iago employs when speaking of Desdemona's sexual union with Othello is in keeping with his earlier sneering reference to Cassio being 'damned in a fair wife' (line 20) and his role as matchmaker for Roderigo. Shakespeare perhaps suggests that Iago is crude and unable to understand love, or loving relationships. This idea is

CHECK THE FILM
In the 1990 film of an RSC production, Brabantio weeps and shouts throughout Act I, and the references to Othello bewitching Desdemona are delivered with a sense of urgency. Altogether, these details make Brabantio a sympathetic figure, whose sense of loss and bewilderment are clear. He moves away, hurt and angry, as Desdemona tries to say farewell to him, refusing to be embraced.

developed later in the play. Iago also seems to be able to choose his words and line of reasoning to suit his audience, so that he has exactly the effect he wishes to have. He talks Roderigo out of his indignation very easily, leading him by the nose throughout this scene; he is equally successful in alarming Brabantio, colouring the old man's view of Othello. Act I Scene 1 establishes Iago as a powerful and manipulative figure, who instigates and stage-manages chaos. He also proves that he is adept at getting himself out of trouble, or avoiding it altogether: Iago knows when to make himself scarce.

This opening scene is laced with **dramatic irony**, all of which centres on Iago. Roderigo fails to see that a man who admits he is a selfish fraud might also be gulling him, and Brabantio is unaware of the aptness of his line, 'Thou art a villain' (line 116). But there is enjoyment to be had in watching the villain at work. He has revealed himself very early and we watch fascinated as he manipulates others. We are also intrigued by the scurrilous descriptions of Othello, because we have also been told that the Moor is an extremely effective soldier, relied on by the Venetian senate as the best man they have (lines 145–51). It seems that *Othello* is going to be concerned with differing or contradictory points of view.

Other key ideas are introduced in the opening scene. Othello's 'otherness' is established through references to him as 'the Moor' (line 39) and 'the thicklips'. Deception is clearly going to be a significant issue; Roderigo initially believes Iago has deceived him, Othello and Desdemona have deceived others by marrying secretly and we know that Iago intends to deceive the Moor in subsequent scenes. Trust is an important issue for all the characters on stage and jealousy already plays a part in events. Iago is jealous of Cassio, and we can presume that Roderigo feels jealous of Othello for 'beating' him to Desdemona. Finally, the different examples of conflict that open and close Act I Scene 1 are accompanied by references to a greater conflict: the invasion of Cyprus.

CONTEXT

The origin of the word Moor is 'Mauri', which refers to the Berbers who lived in the Roman province of Mauritania, in North Africa. Berbers range in colour from very dark to blond and blue-eyed. For this reason, critics are divided about Othello's skin colour.

GLOSSARY

9	**Off-capped** showed respect by removing hats
13	**epithets** terms or phrases
24	**toged** wearing official dress (togas worn by Roman senators were the garb of peace)
30	**counter-caster** accountant
38	**affined** bound
47	**cashiered** dismissed or cast off
74	**timorous** frightening
98	**distempering** exciting
110	**Barbary horse** Arabian thoroughbred (this reference is designed to evoke Othello's barbarism)
112	**jennets** small Spanish horses
156	**Sagittary** the house where Othello and Desdemona are staying, named after the sign of Sagittarius, the centaur

CONTEXT

At the beginning of the play, Othello's situation is that of the hero of a comedy, not a tragedy. He is the secret, successful suitor to an approving and willing young woman, whose father is enraged by the relationship. This sort of romantic tangle is common in comedies of the period, including Shakespeare's *The Taming of the Shrew*. Cuckoldry was a plot device often used in comedy e.g. *The Merry Wives of Windsor*.

SCENE 2

- Othello is called to the Venetian council on urgent military business.
- Brabantio accuses Othello of bewitching his daughter.

The second scene opens half way through another conversation involving Iago. Again there is a sense of conflict. Iago appears to be recounting the events of the previous scene to Othello, emphasising the insulting way that Othello has been spoken of and Brabantio's negative reaction to his daughter's marriage. Iago (hypocritically) insists that he wished to revenge the insults to the general, but Othello is not perturbed. When Iago warns him that Brabantio is a popular figure who may use his influence to have the marriage overturned and Othello pursued by the law, he dismisses these concerns. Othello is confident that his services to the state, his reputation and his royal breeding will speak for him. He also emphasises the strength of his love for Desdemona.

What contribution do the early scenes in Venice make to the play?

When Iago hears someone approaching he advises the general to go inside. Othello replies that he 'must be found' (line 30): he has nothing to be ashamed of. Cassio enters with a message from the Duke, who urgently requires Othello's presence at a meeting of the Venetian council. Several messengers have been sent to find Othello, suggesting his importance to the state. Othello goes into the house to speak to someone. Iago informs Cassio of Othello's marriage and then, when Othello returns, the soldiers set out for the council meeting. They have not gone very far when they are accosted by Brabantio and his followers, who are armed with swords. Othello commands the men to put away their weapons and responds with dignity to Brabantio's accusations of evil enchantment. The senator urges his followers to seize the 'thief' (line 57) who has stolen his daughter. Othello warns them against laying hands on him and offers to answer Brabantio's accusations. Brabantio says that he would like to see him imprisoned but is then informed that Othello has been summoned on state business. Brabantio decides to go to the council meeting too, so that his fellow senators and the Duke can be informed of Othello's treacherous behaviour. He insists that his own domestic troubles are 'not an idle cause' (line 95).

COMMENTARY

Further conflict unfolds in this second scene. Our suspicions about Iago are confirmed by his first lines, and by his oath at line 33. His pretended loyalty and indignation are designed to evoke trust and favourable opinion, as is his false self-deprecation. Iago's anxiety about Othello's welfare is hypocritical. However, all his remarks up to line 17 are entirely plausible. Iago focuses on issues that *will* trouble Othello. In contrast to all the characters we have seen so far, Othello speaks with a measured calm in his first speeches. His quiet confidence and obvious sincerity about his love for Desdemona are immediately attractive. We realise that Othello is not the pompous creature described in the previous scene and that, in spite of his clandestine marriage, he prefers to be open about his actions (lines 30–2). Othello is also brave, dignified and authoritative, as shown by his handling of Brabantio and his followers. We may accuse him of pride when he speaks of his services to the state and insists that his 'parts … title, and … perfect soul' (line 31) will 'manifest me rightly' (line 32), but we understand that his reputation has been attacked. By the time that Brabantio launches his verbal assault on Othello at line 62 we will probably feel enough sympathy for the general to sense that Brabantio's accusations are not entirely justified. Finally, this scene shows that Othello and Iago are polar opposites; one seeks to diffuse conflict while the other revels in it.

GLOSSARY		
7	**scurvy** insulting, rude	
12	**magnifico** a title used of Brabantio	
17	**cable** scope (a nautical metaphor)	
18	**signiory** the Venetian state/ oligarchy	
21	**promulgate** make known or publish	
26	**unhoused** unconfined, free	
33	**Janus** the two faced Roman god of beginnings, doorways and passages	
50	**land carrack** either a treasure ship or a slang term for a prostitute	
95	**idle** unimportant or trivial	

SCENE 3

- The senate discuss the war with the Turks.
- Othello answers Brabantio's accusations and is sent to Cyprus on a military campaign.
- Iago starts to plan his revenge against Othello.

We move to the council chamber, where the Duke and the Venetian senators discuss conflicting reports about the movements of the Turkish fleet. After receiving further information from the commander in Cyprus (Montano) it seems clear that the Turks intend to attack that island. When Othello and Brabantio enter, the Duke immediately tells Othello to prepare to go to war. He welcomes Brabantio and tells him that his presence was sorely missed at the meeting. Brabantio is more concerned with his private troubles and repeats his accusations against Othello. The meeting to

CONTEXT

By the time that Shakespeare came to write *Othello*, Venice had been employing paid mercenaries and freelance generals – who had their own armies – to protect the wealth of the city for quite some time.

discuss military operations and strategy now becomes a trial of Othello. The Duke asks Othello to respond to the charges against him and we hear conflicting reports of his 'whole course of love' (line 92). Brabantio insists again that his daughter must have been bewitched, while Othello maintains that he won her love fairly. He asks that Desdemona be brought to the council chamber to confirm the truth of his words. While attendants fetch her, Othello continues to offer his version of their courtship, which the Duke finally accepts, urging Brabantio to reconcile himself to the marriage. Brabantio refuses to believe that his daughter could be 'half the wooer' (line 176).

Desdemona's polite but firm insistence that she now owes her love and duty to her husband confirms Othello's version of their courtship. Brabantio is bitterly disappointed and finds it impossible to accept Othello as a son-in-law. The Duke tries to persuade him to make the best of things and not cause further mischief, but Brabantio remains angry. He brushes off the Duke's conciliatory words and compares his loss of Desdemona with the possible loss of Cyprus to the Turks. The Duke takes this opportunity to return to military business and tells Othello to prepare to depart for Cyprus. Desdemona asks to be allowed to accompany her husband. Othello insists that her presence will not distract him from military affairs and places his wife in Iago's charge. Just before he leaves with the senators, the Duke makes a final attempt at consoling Brabantio, but the old man turns sourly to Othello and warns him against trusting Desdemona; she has deceived her father and may one day deceive him. Othello replies that he trusts his wife's 'faith' unquestioningly (line 295).

CHECK THE BOOK

For Iago's characterisation as 'motiveless malignity' see Coleridge's comments in John Wain (ed.), *Othello: Casebook.*

The act closes as it began, with Iago and Roderigo in conversation. Roderigo is despondent and says that he will drown himself since he can no longer hope to win Desdemona. Iago is impatient with this sort of foolish, defeatist talk and tries to persuade Roderigo that Desdemona will soon look elsewhere for love when she is sated with Othello's body. He argues that the romance had a violent commencement and therefore cannot last. Roderigo is cheered by this idea and falls in with Iago's plan; he will gather his resources together and accompany Iago to the Cyprus wars. Alone on stage

Iago reveals his true motives. He is toying with Roderigo 'for my sport and profit' (line 385) and suspects Othello of cuckolding him: he wants revenge. He is determined to oust Cassio and take his place and muses about the best way to achieve his aims. He decides that he can easily abuse Othello's honest and trusting nature and will try to persuade him that Cassio is too familiar with Desdemona. As the scene closes, Iago is very satisfied with his half-formed plots; he looks forward to putting his ideas into action.

COMMENTARY

Conflict and conflicting views and opinions dominate Act I Scene 3 as they have dominated the other two scenes in Act I. The Duke attempts to steer a wise course in matters of love and war, but Brabantio's sour exit and Iago's final soliloquy suggest that Othello's marriage will not proceed as smoothly as the couple expect it to. At this stage, in spite of the opprobrium of Brabantio and the fact that Othello is forced to explain and justify his actions, the two lovers seem utterly secure in each other's affection. Othello is confident that his wife will back him up early in the scene, and she later refuses to be parted from him. From Othello's description of the courtship it appears that Desdemona was indeed 'half the wooer' (line 176) so it does not come as a surprise to hear her say she 'did love the Moor to live with him' (line 249). Both Desdemona and Othello speak plainly and movingly about their affection for one another in this scene.

What are the origins of their love? Othello says that Desdemona 'loved me for the dangers I had passed / And I loved her that she did pity them' (lines 168–9). Desdemona was seduced by Othello's story-telling powers, while the Moor was enchanted by the Venetian's sympathetic response to his history. There is no question of their ardent sincerity, but we might wonder whether each perhaps fell in love with an image or idea of the other. We may also choose to question how realistic Othello is about love. He professes that he has had little experience in matters of the heart. He is eloquent when describing his experiences as a soldier, but needed prompting to woo Desdemona and seems to expect to be able to continue his military duties without any distractions. He is firm and confident about this: love and war can be combined.

CONTEXT

Renaissance Venice was renowned for several things. It was a cosmopolitan place, where personal advancement was possible, in spite of the rigid and hierarchical social structure that existed. Travellers admired Venice because of the sensual pleasures the city provided. While the Venetians were considered hospitable, they also had a reputation for religious zeal.

Othello's military prowess is established early in the scene by the urgent discussions between the senators, while Desdemona's domestic qualities are emphasised by Brabantio and Othello's descriptions of her. Now Othello has to negotiate the domestic sphere too. Are we to make anything of the fact that Othello is a mature man, coming late to love, while Brabantio suggests that his daughter is not much more than a girl? Will this be another cause of conflict in the play? We may feel that Othello's speech at line 261 is a little naïve. Here Othello seems to be denying the sexual element of his relationship with Desdemona, insisting that his identity as soldier comes before anything else. Iago's contemptuous descriptions of Othello in this scene are troublesome but perhaps almost plausible, given the general's words and actions. We may admire Othello's 'free and open nature' (line 398), but we may also be concerned that the general is indeed trusting enough to be led by the nose (after all, Desdemona ensnared him with her 'world of sighs', line 160). His decision to place his wife in Iago's care is alarming, although it indicates his high opinion of his ensign. We receive two ominous hints about the future progress of Othello's marriage when the senators leave; Brabantio warns Othello against trusting Desdemona, while the first senator tells Othello to 'use Desdemona well' (line 292). These lines are examples of **dramatic irony**, hints to the audience about the way the plot will develop.

The theme of deception is continued in this scene. Like Iago, the Turks have been successful in concealing their intentions. Brabantio's assessment of his daughter's character has proved to be false and his own affection for Othello has been revealed as superficial. Iago's soliloquy suggests that the manipulation of Roderigo and Othello in the first act is a prelude to more serious deception; the web Iago is weaving will ensnare Desdemona and Cassio too. It is entirely appropriate that Iago refers to hell and night in his last two lines. He is devilish. Note his ability to improvise swiftly; at the start of his soliloquy he has not decided how he is going to proceed with his revenge. A few lines later he has the outline of a workable and subtle plan.

CHECK THE BOOK

For comments on the Venetian setting, see the chapter on *Othello* in John Russell Brown's *Shakespeare: The Tragedies*.

GLOSSARY

1	**composition** consistency
19	**assay** test
25	**warlike brace** state of military preparedness
31	**wake and wage** stir up and engage in battle
36	**injointed** united or joined with
62	**mountebanks** charlatans or quacks
65	**Sans** without
199	**clogs** shackles used on animals to prevent them from straying
201	**grise** step
217	**gall** bitterness
225	**sufficiency** worth, ability
227	**slubber** sully or besmear
232	**agnize** acknowledge, recognise
234	**hardness** hardship
238	**exhibition** financial support
274	**indign** unworthy
306	**incontinently** at once
333	**sect or scion** branch or graft
339	**perdurable** eternal
350	**acerb** bitter
350	**coloquintida** a bitter apple used as a purgative
372	**Traverse** get ready for action (a military term)
384	**snipe** a bird this is a term of contempt like 'woodcock'

CHECK THE BOOK

For literary sources of *Othello*, see Kenneth Muir, *The Sources of Shakespeare's Plays*.

ACT II

SCENE 1

- The Turkish fleet is destroyed by the storm.
- Othello, Desdemona and Iago arrive safely in Cyprus.
- Iago involves Roderigo in his plan to discredit Cassio.

The scene moves to Cyprus, where the island's governor, Montano and two gentlemen anxiously await Othello's arrival. Because of a storm they cannot see clearly what is happening. This confusion mirrors the confusion of the first act. Montano's concern also indicates his respect for Othello and reinforces our esteem for the Moor; he is looked upon as Cyprus's saviour. The storm is also a device by which Shakespeare can dispose of the Turkish threat, which is no longer necessary to the plot. The focus of *Othello* is to be the general's marriage and Iago's attempts to undermine it.

A gentleman announces that the Turkish fleet has been destroyed by the tempest and also informs Montano that Cassio's ship has arrived safely. When he enters it is clear that Cassio is also concerned about Othello's safety, but he reassures Montano that the Moor's ship is strong and its captain a reliable and experienced sailor. News of the sighting of another ship is brought in. Cassio sends a gentleman to find out who is landing and informs Montano of Othello's recent marriage, praising Desdemona's virtues. We learn that it is Iago's ship which has landed. The ensign enters, escorting his wife Emilia and Desdemona. Cassio greets them graciously. Desdemona immediately asks after her husband and is disturbed to hear that his ship has not yet come in. Another ship is sighted and while we wait to find out whose it is, Desdemona attempts to distract herself in conversation with the others. She discusses women and their characters with Iago, whose opinion of the fair sex is far from flattering. The ensign says – in a light-hearted tone – that women are talkative, indiscreet, lascivious and deceitful. Desdemona takes him to task for his ungenerous comments, while Cassio excuses Iago's soldierly bluntness. It appears that Cassio touches Desdemona's hand at this point – a gesture of courtesy – because Iago informs us in an aside that he will use Cassio's innocent gallantry against him.

Othello's trumpet is heard and the Moor himself finally arrives. He and Desdemona greet each other warmly and Othello expresses his great satisfaction at seeing his wife again; he says he could die happily at this moment. The couple's joy is undermined by an another aside from Iago, who remarks sourly that their mutual happiness will not last because he will set the couple at odds. The general then leaves for the castle, accompanied by all the other characters, except Iago and Roderigo. Iago now enlists Roderigo's help in his plan to discredit Cassio. He convinces Roderigo that Desdemona is in love with Cassio, and that Roderigo's only chance of gaining her affections is to disgrace the lieutenant. Roderigo is reluctant to believe that Desdemona is as wanton as Iago suggests, but allows himself to be persuaded that it is natural that she should tire of Othello so quickly. He agrees to find an occasion to provoke Cassio into losing his temper later that evening. Iago is left alone on stage and offers us further insight into his motives. His hatred of Othello is combined with contempt for a 'constant, loving, noble nature' (line 287). He reiterates his desire to be revenged on the Moor and his suspicions of having been cuckolded. Iago even suggests that Cassio has cuckolded him.

CHECK THE BOOK

For a positive reading of Othello's character as a lover, see Helen Gardner's comments in John Wain (ed.), *Othello: Casebook*.

COMMENTARY

The principal characters are now isolated in Cyprus, removed from the orderly social and political scene of Venice. In this new and unfamiliar setting Iago is able to prey on all those around him. The storm reflects the passions that will be unleashed in this new setting. We might also see the storm as being related to Othello and his emotions in particular; he is associated with sea imagery throughout the play. Until Othello lands safely the mood of all the characters on stage is uneasy. But while the Moor's appearance calms their fears, it is impossible for the audience to relax because of Iago's asides, soliloquy and dialogue with Roderigo. Iago's cynicism undermines and taints the innocence, relief and joy of the other characters. Ironically, the ensign is even able to speak in an openly cynical and misogynistic way in this scene and take others in; he plays the role of bluff soldier in his exchange with Desdemona. This is a mark of his power; when he is most 'honest', Iago is disbelieved or thought to be entertaining. We might also view his crude delineation of the female character as a sign of Iago's narrow and twisted nature. Unlike Othello, who takes delight in his wife's presence, Iago can only see women as false, mean spirited and inferior creatures. His misogynistic opinions are developed further in his soliloquy, when he speaks disparagingly of Desdemona. The differences between Othello and Iago's characters become even more glaring if we compare Othello's words and actions with Iago's. Othello's speeches are generous, relaxed, joyful: Iago is full of hate and contempt. He speaks of lust, preferment and profit. His – some would say surprising – admission of 'love' (line 289) for Desdemona is intriguing. As if recognising that the word 'love' does not suit him, Iago immediately redefines his feeling as 'lust', 'partly led to diet my revenge' (line 292). Personal and professional jealousy dominate Iago's soliloquy. He wants Othello to suffer the same torment that rages inside him. At the moment the male protagonists could not be more different in situation or impulse, although we might feel that this scene confirms that both men are prey to very powerful emotions: love and hate. Would you agree with critics who suggest that there is an undertone of competitive racism in Iago's soliloquy, that he cannot accept that Desdemona, a wealthy aristocratic white woman, has chosen a black man?

It is important to note that Othello greets Desdemona before moving on to speak to Montano and the other soldiers garrisoned at Cyprus; love is put before war, signalling the domestic focus of the tragedy. Othello also suggests that Desdemona is his source of happiness now; he seems almost overwhelmed by this feeling at lines 187–91 and 193–7. Shakespeare is emphasising the all-encompassing nature of his love in order to prepare us for his titanic jealousy later in the play. This scene also provides Iago with the first piece of false proof he can use to poison Othello's mind: Cassio's gallantry. The lieutenant has not yet emerged as a fully drawn character, although we see from his behaviour in this scene that he possesses the social graces required to fit the role of lover Iago has cast him in.

CHECK THE NET

For an essay on race and religion and other *Othello* materials, including links between *Othello* and *The Merchant of Venice*, see A Masterpiece Theatre web site: **www.pbs.org/wgbh/masterpiece/othello**.

GLOSSARY		
9	**mortoise** joint	
14	**burning bear** a star, the Little Bear, used by sailors when navigating	
18	**embayed** protected by a bay	
23	**wrack and sufferance** destruction, damage	
48	**pilot** captain	
63	**quirks** extravagant conceits or praise	
77	**A se'nnight's** by a week	

126	**birdlime** a substance spread on bushes to snare birds
126	**frieze** woollen fabric
155	**To change the cod's head for the salmon's tail** to make an unwise exchange
176	**clyster-pipes** a syringe for enemas or vaginal douches
216	**the court of guard** guard house
236	**conscionable** to behave well so as to have a clear conscience
307	**egregiously** extraordinarily (bad)

SCENE 2

- Peace is restored in Cyprus.
- There is to be a night of revels to celebrate Othello's marriage.

In this short scene a herald confirms the destruction of the Turkish fleet and prepares us for the celebration and consummation of Othello and Desdemona's marriage.

COMMENTARY

The herald's joyful proclamation marks a return to civil order. However, the audience is aware that the peace will shortly be disrupted by Iago, who will take advantage of Othello's generosity. Again, there is an explicit linking of private emotions and public life, as in Act I Scene 3.

CONTEXT

The subject matter of *Othello* would have appealed to James I, who wrote a poem 'Lepanto', about the 1571 battle when Christian forces destroyed a Turkish fleet.

GLOSSARY

| 3 | *mere perdition* complete destruction |
| 8 | **All offices are open** all the kitchens and cellars are open (for drinking and eating) |

SCENE 3

- On the night of the wedding celebrations, Cassio is dismissed from his post for fighting when drunk on duty.
- Cassio bemoans his loss of status.

CHECK THE FILM
Compare different versions of the drinking scene. In the 1990 TV production, Iago prepares a potent punch, and leads the singing; but he does not force Cassio to drink. The drinking game is essentially good humoured, and Cassio chooses to consume a lot of alcohol. In Parker's 1995 film, Cassio is much more reluctant to drink, and has to be prompted and offered wine by Iago, who uses gestures and tone of voice to insinuate that Cassio is not a 'real man' if he fails to drink his share.

We move to the castle, where Othello instructs Cassio to ensure that the festivities remain under control. Cassio confidently tells him that Iago is in charge; both general and lieutenant believe that 'honest' (line 6) Iago is both reliable and capable. Desdemona and Othello leave to consummate their marriage, bidding Cassio goodnight.

When Iago enters Cassio immediately wishes to set out to the watch, but the ensign persuades him that there is still time to enjoy the revels. The two men discuss Desdemona. Iago urges the lieutenant to drink some more wine. Out of courtesy Cassio reluctantly agrees; he says he has a poor head for drink and has already taken enough. While Cassio steps out to call in some of the Cyprus gallants, Iago reveals that he intends to make Cassio drunk so that it will be easy to provoke him into quarrelling. He intends that Cassio – and others – will disturb the peace. Cassio returns with Montano and the high-spirited carousing continues. Cassio lapses into drunkenness. After a while he decides to attend to his duties, maintaining stoutly that he is sober as he leaves. Iago makes a point of telling Montano that Cassio is an habitual drunk, unsettling the governor, who says that Othello should be informed of his lieutenant's weakness. Roderigo makes a brief appearance but is soon hurried off the stage by Iago, who urges him to follow and antagonise Cassio.

A few moments later these two return; Roderigo is driven in by an angry Cassio, who strikes his adversary. Montano tries to part them, but is drawn into a fight with Cassio himself. Iago tells Roderigo to cause further chaos and panic by running about the town crying 'Mutiny!' An alarm bell rings and Othello arrives. Iago immediately assumes the role of mediator and pacifier. He initially pretends that he does not know how the altercation began. Cassio is too ashamed to speak and Montano, wounded and breathless, refers the general to Iago for an account of the brawl.

So it is left to the ancient to provide the increasingly angry Othello with a description of the night's events. With pretended reluctance he recounts details of Cassio's assault on Montano. The lieutenant is immediately dismissed from his post. At this point Desdemona enters. Othello protectively sweeps her away, commenting that it is part of a soldier's life to have his rest disturbed by strife. Before he leaves he makes sure that Montano's wounds are attended to and puts Iago in charge of restoring calm in the town.

Iago and Cassio are left on stage. Cassio is utterly wretched about the loss of his reputation, and disgusted with his own behaviour. Iago offers him advice. He suggests seeking Desdemona's assistance. If she will plead for him, Cassio is sure be restored to Othello's favour. Like Roderigo before him, Cassio is persuaded that 'honest' Iago has his best interests at heart and leaves, satisfied that the ancient's proposal is sound. Iago turns triumphantly to the audience; who can accuse him of villainy when he offers such helpful, wise advice? He now informs us that he will convince Othello that Desdemona pleads for Cassio because she is in love with him.

CHECK THE NET
For lists of resources on the web and gateways to further resources visit **www.is.bham.ac. uk/shakespeare**.

Roderigo returns, a rather pathetic figure. He has been beaten soundly. Worse, he has nothing to show for his financial outlay and is as far from securing Desdemona's affections as he was in Venice. He intends to return home. This does not suit Iago, who still needs Roderigo. The ensign persuades him to stay; he should not be so impatient, he should think less of his bruises and more of his achievements; after all, he has this evening 'cashiered' his rival (line 370). Iago sends Roderigo back to his billet and muses on, alone. His next move will be to enlist his innocent wife's help; Emilia must promote Cassio's cause with Desdemona while he poisons Othello's mind.

COMMENTARY

In this scene Iago's ideas becomes reality. He continues to manipulate the hapless Roderigo effortlessly; at the end of the scene

CONTEXT

The portrayal of Iago demonstrates some of the Elizabethans' misunderstandings of the works of the Florentine writer, Niccolo Machiavelli (1469–1527). Today Machiavelli is respected as a political and social theorist, but Shakespeare and his contemporaries believed that his ideas were immoral. So they created stage **Machiavels** who were devious and unscrupulous. In works such as *The Prince*, Machiavelli sought to discuss what rulers *actually did* when they were in government, as well as what *they should do*.

he is confident enough to usher his stooge off with an impatient and contemptuous 'Nay, get thee gone' (line 377). Iago acknowledges that speed is vital if his plan is to work, although he is willing to spend time smoothing the way; he draws Cassio out and then reassures him that he must not give up hope (this is exactly the tactic he has used with Roderigo). In the first two acts we see the methods that Iago will use on Othello work to devastating effect on lesser men. The ensign is sharpening his weapons. Here we see him exploit the limitations or weaknesses of Cassio and Roderigo. Soon he will prey on a much nobler victim.

At all times Iago acts as if he has someone else's interests at heart. He also presents himself in the best possible light; for example, in the aftermath of the brawl he pretends to be reluctant to accuse Cassio. Not only does this make him look like a loyal friend (he needs Cassio to trust him), but it is also the most effective way of convincing Othello that his lieutenant has behaved disgracefully. Othello, who prefers openness and honesty, is forced to demand the truth, which angers him. However, he appreciates Iago's false 'protection' of Cassio. We see Iago's true malignity in his soliloquy at line 331, when he states very clearly that he intends to use Desdemona's goodness to 'enmesh them all' (line 357). He now seeks the destruction of an innocent, with whom he has no quarrel. We also see Iago's delight in his own cunning in this speech; he revels in the fact that he has the power to turn Desdemona's 'virtue into pitch' (line 355). As in previous scenes, Iago shows nothing but contempt for honesty and innocence and looks forward to defiling them. Even his wife is to be used in his plan. Iago's only loyalty is to himself. His appeal to the audience at lines 331–4 shows him revelling in his own acting abilities. His imagery is crude and materialistic; he will convince Othello that his wife pleads for Cassio 'for her body's lust' (line 352); she will 'undo her credit with the Moor' (line 354). With Othello and Cassio Iago is generally more polite and circumspect. Part of Iago's success lies in the fact that he tells his victims what they want to hear, or uses the arguments that are most likely to win them over to his way of thinking. He can talk Roderigo and Cassio round because they want to be comforted and provided with solutions to their difficulties. Another example of Iago's duplicity comes in his use of the word 'think', which anticipates his manipulation of Othello's thoughts. He toys with Cassio when he says, 'I think you think I love you' (line 306). The audience will be alarmed by this double dealing.

In this scene Othello's control is undermined, although the general is as yet unaware that he is being manipulated. Iago disrupts both his wedding night and the peace of the town with great efficiency. Othello speaks with his customary authority, but we know that his power to rule himself and others has been threatened. The importance Cassio places on his reputation reflects Othello's pride in his own honour, which is also to be destroyed by Iago.

GLOSSARY		
51	**pottle-deep**	at the bottom of a two quart tankard
61	**a rouse**	large draught of drink
65	**cannikin**	small drinking can
73	**potent in potting**	mighty drinkers
78	**Almain**	German
88	**lown**	lout
136	**ingraft**	deeply ingrained
150	**mazzard**	head
157	**Diablo!**	what the devil!
202	**collied**	clouded

CHECK THE FILM
In the RSC 1990 film, Roderigo is portrayed as an hysterical young man, who weeps and flails on the ground when he realises Othello's marriage to Desdemona will not be dissolved. Ian McKellen's Iago has a good deal of authority over him from the start. He treats Roderigo like a child. After the drunken brawl, Iago picks Roderigo up, strokes his head, dusts him down and dresses his wounds. He is not genuinely kind, however; sometimes he barks orders and advice, which frightens Roderigo.

ACT III

SCENE 1

- Cassio hires some musicians to serenade the bride and groom.
- Emilia agrees to take Cassio to speak with Desdemona.

The following morning Cassio hires musicians to perform some music to celebrate Othello and Desdemona's marriage. It appears that the music does not please Othello because he sends a clown to

CHECK THE FILM

Ian McKellen's Iago is a man motivated by sexual jealousy. He is possessive of his wife, kissing and putting his arms around her when he arrives in Cyprus. He also watches Emilia's behaviour with Cassio closely. We can see why he might believe he has been cuckolded. When they greet each other, Cassio kisses Emilia affectionately on the cheek.

pay them to leave. Cassio then entreats the clown to tell Desdemona's lady-in-waiting, Emilia, that he would like to speak with her. As the clown leaves, Iago makes his entrance. Cassio is pleased to see him and grateful when Iago says he will ensure that his wife attends him presently. Iago also says he will help Cassio by diverting Othello's attention so that Cassio can speak to Desdemona alone. When Emilia arrives we learn that Othello and Desdemona have already been discussing Cassio's case and that Desdemona has defended Cassio. Emilia agrees to take Cassio to speak with Desdemona.

COMMENTARY

This brief scene furthers the plot. We have an impression that time is moving swiftly and that the action of the play is continuous. Emilia's sincerity and her obvious closeness to Desdemona are appealing, but we know that she is unwittingly helping her husband and not Cassio when she agrees to take the latter to speak with her mistress. The scene is laced with heavy and ominous irony; Cassio's words at lines 40–1 are chilling for the audience, who know that the opposite of what he says about Iago is true. Note that it is Iago's suggestion that Cassio speak alone with Desdemona; the lieutenant had intended to plead through Emilia. We know that there is little chance of his reinstatement: Cassio's optimism makes him a slightly pathetic figure. Observe how Iago contrives – as usual – to arrive on the scene at an opportune moment.

GLOSSARY	
23	**quillets** from 'quidlibet', a lawyer's verbal quibble

SCENE 2

- Othello sets out to inspect 'the works'.

In this brief scene Othello is busy with official business; he intends to inspect the fortifications in the town, with his loyal deputy Iago at his side.

COMMENTARY

This scene is as **ironic** as the previous one; while the innocent Othello is absorbed in military matters, his personal affairs are being steadily undermined (we assume that Cassio will take this opportunity to speak to Desdemona, thus falling into the trap that Iago has laid for him). Othello is probably also acting in accordance with Iago's plan to 'draw the Moor / Out of the way' (III.1.37–8) when he agrees to tour 'the works' (line 3). The first two scenes of Act III prepare us for the ensign's assault on his commander in Act III Scene 3, which is the central scene of *Othello*.

GLOSSARY	
1	pilot captain
3	works fortifications

CHECK THE BOOK

For comments on the historical context of the play, see Nicholas Potter *'Othello' – A Reader's Guide to Essential Criticism*.

SCENE 3

- Desdemona pleads with Othello to reinstate Cassio.
- Iago convinces Othello that his wife is in love with Cassio.

In contrast to the previous two scenes, this scene is lengthy. Here we watch as Othello's mind is poisoned. The tight focus is not only psychologically convincing; it also aids the impression that time is moving swiftly (favouring Iago).

Desdemona and Emilia offer Cassio their assurances that Othello will soon restore him to favour. Desdemona insists that she will talk her husband 'out of patience' (line 23) until he agrees to reinstate Cassio. Othello enters with Iago. Uneasy and ashamed, Cassio declines to stay when Desdemona offers to plead for him there and then. Iago immediately sets to work, observing briefly that he does not like the manner of Cassio's leave-taking. Desdemona enters. She speaks her mind without any hesitation, urging her husband to call Cassio back and reinstate him. Othello is reluctant to discuss this subject, but Desdemona is undaunted, demanding (playfully but in a determined way) to know when Cassio will be returned to favour. Othello asks to be left 'a little to myself' (line 85), but agrees that he is willing to see Cassio 'when he will' (III.3.75). Desdemona has to be satisfied with this and obediently takes her leave with Emilia. Othello says he will join her shortly.

Iago continues to disparage Cassio, suggesting in a roundabout way that he suspects him of false behaviour with Desdemona. Iago hints that the conversation Othello interrupted at the start of the scene was not as innocent as it may have appeared. By pretending to be reluctant to articulate his suspicions, Iago encourages Othello to question what he has observed. He urges his master *not* to be jealous, without telling him directly why he *should* be jealous. Othello insists that he is not given to jealousy, but his mind has clearly been moving in the very direction Iago intended because he then speaks of his wife's attributes and talents. Othello brings up the subject of rivalry himself when he says 'she had eyes and chose me' (line 192). We begin to sense that the Moor is deceiving himself when he says 'there is no more but this: / Away at once with love or jealousy!' (lines 194–5).

CHECK THE NET

'Mr William Shakespeare and the Internet' is an excellent guide to the best sites on the Internet on Shakespeare, including general criticism. Visit **http://shakespeare. palomar.edu**.

Iago knows he has ensnared his victim. He now chooses to drive home the advantage he has gained, offering Othello specific advice; watch Desdemona with Cassio, remember that Venetian women are deceitful. The ensign reminds Othello that his wife has already deceived her father. This is a profitable line of argument for Iago, who sees immediately that the Moor is troubled by what he has heard. Iago twists the knife, pointing out that Desdemona refused a number of natural matrimonial choices before marrying Othello and is now perhaps only 'recoiling to her better judgement' (line 240) by feeling attracted to Cassio. We know that Othello has played right into Iago's hands when he asks him to set Emilia spying on Desdemona. His plaintive and rather helpless question when he is briefly left alone on stage – 'Why did I marry?' (line 245) – shows Othello's perturbation and misery. He is now plagued by doubt.

Iago is merciless. He returns swiftly to offer further wicked advice: hold Cassio at arm's length for a while and observe how Desdemona reacts to this. Alone at last, Othello considers what he has heard. He doubts himself momentarily (he is black, old, rude of speech) and seems bewildered by how to proceed. He cannot quite bring himself to believe that his wife is false, although much of his soliloquy is taken up with the idea of establishing proof that Desdemona has deceived him. His wife appears and reminds him that 'the generous islanders' (line 284) await him at dinner. When Othello responds briefly and faintly, Desdemona recognises at once that something is amiss. She offers to bind her husband's aching head with a handkerchief, but Othello will not be comforted and suggests that they go in together. In her anxiety Desdemona does not realise that she has dropped her handkerchief, which is picked up by Emilia, who comes in after the couple have left. Emilia informs us that the 'napkin' (line 294) was Desdemona's first gift from her husband and that Iago has been pestering her to steal it for some time. Iago chooses an opportune moment to reappear. He is delighted when Emilia gives him the handkerchief but refuses to tell her how he will use it. When Emilia leaves we learn more about Iago's nefarious intentions. The handkerchief will be left at Cassio's lodgings to serve as proof of his secret liaison with Desdemona.

Othello returns, absorbed with thoughts of his wife's treachery. He now seems absolutely convinced that Desdemona is guilty of deceiving him and is tormented by the lack of evidence. At the same time Othello also seems to regret his suspicions; he says that he was happy when he was ignorant of 'her stolen hours of lust' (line 341). His says that his peace of mind is destroyed forever. Othello wants 'ocular proof' (line 363) of his wife's adultery. As he talks he becomes increasingly agitated, swinging between doubt and conviction; at one moment he seems angry with Iago for telling him of his suspicions; then he is sure that his wife's lasciviousness has ruined his reputation. He is, as Iago observes, 'eaten up with passion' (line 394). Iago feeds Othello's jealousy by pointing out that it will be difficult to obtain evidence (employing some coarse descriptions of Desdemona and Cassio's lust) and then by offering a tantalising description of an occasion on which he shared Cassio's bed; the lieutenant apparently called out to Desdemona in his sleep and attempted to kiss and fondle his bed mate (Iago), mistaking him for the object of his desire. This 'dream' (line 431) disturbs Othello greatly; his thoughts turn immediately to violent revenge. Iago then

CHECK THE FILM
Iago's brutality towards his wife is emphasised in Oliver Parker's 1995 film. During the scene when Emilia gives Iago Desdemona's handkerchief, the villain is lying on top of, and hurting, his wife.

CHECK THE NET

The site 'Shakespeare's Moor: The Sources and Representations' has detailed information about the way Moors were portrayed in the Elizabethan and Jacobean eras. Find it at **www. geocities.com/ Wellesley/7261/ gripe5**.

moves on to his pièce de résistance: the handkerchief. He tells the general that he has seen Cassio wiping his beard with it. Kneeling, Othello vows never to look back again; he is utterly consumed by 'bloody thoughts' (line 460). Iago kneels with him and pledges his allegiance to 'wronged Othello's service' (line 470). His 'loyalty' is welcomed by the desperate Moor, who asks him to kill Cassio. Iago then receives the promotion he has been hankering after; he is made lieutenant when he agrees to murder his 'friend' Cassio (line 476). The scene ends on a sinister note; Othello leaves, intending to 'furnish me with some swift means of death / For the fair devil' (lines 480–1) while Iago repeats his false protestation of unswerving loyalty.

COMMENTARY

The progress of Act III Scene 3 is painful to behold. Everything proceeds exactly as Iago wishes. The audience knows from the outset that Desdemona will doom herself with every utterance. We recognise the horrible irony of her remark that she would rather die than abandon her commitment to plead for Cassio and then wince as she carries out her promise. Cassio's innocent uneasiness goes against him, as Desdemona's forthright approach goes against her; all because of Iago's deceptively short and simple opening line, 'Ha, I like not that' (line 34). Their honesty is no match for his duplicity.

In the first part of the scene we watch as the ensign and Desdemona try to persuade Othello to adopt their own particular view of Cassio. Their methods of persuasion could not be more different. Desdemona speaks urgently and energetically, praising Cassio and repeating her demand to know exactly when he will be reinstated. She is open and confident. It is possible to interpret her insistence as nagging, and Desdemona is perhaps foolish to keep on with her defence of Cassio when it is clear that Othello does not wish to discuss the matter. We might also accuse Desdemona of meddling in affairs that don't concern her (earlier in the play Othello made it plain that military and domestic life were not to be confused). But why should Desdemona not speak her mind? She has every reason to feel confident of her husband's devotion. We also recognise that her motives for speaking are generous and honest. Desdemona thinks that she is acting in her husband's best interests; Cassio was a 'go between' when Othello and she were courting and he has been a reliable and loyal lieutenant and friend. And she also knows he is genuinely penitent.

Iago's methods are altogether more subtle. His pretended reluctance to speak (which worked so well in Act II Scene 3) enables him to gain ground swiftly. Unlike Desdemona, Iago needs prompting to reveal his thoughts and says very little at the start of the scene. However, the words he chooses are devastatingly effective (see lines 34, 36, 38–40). He is also wise *and* lucky. To a certain extent, as we have seen above, Desdemona 'digs her own grave' by nagging her husband about Cassio, whose exit at the start of the scene could easily be misconstrued. When Iago speaks again after Desdemona's exit he asks a leading question and hints at his own bad thoughts. Note the way in which Iago loads the words 'think' and 'honest'; Desdemona's repeated pleas to know exactly when Cassio will be reinstated irritated Othello; a few minutes later the repetition of these two words has the same effect. The audience will be alert to the fact that these two words are the 'key' to *Othello*. Iago's power resides in these words: he poisons thought by posing as an honest man.

The horrible **irony** of the scene continues. Othello did not want his wife to share her honest thoughts with him and asked her (albeit politely) to leave him alone; now he is impatient for Iago to reveal his (false and evil) thoughts. Iago is not only reluctant to give voice to his thoughts, he also says that he hopes his suspicions are unjustified (lines 147–57). It is interesting to note, however, that Othello makes Iago's task easier; the Moor introduces the subject of his wife himself when he is warned in general terms about jealousy. Iago may indeed be suggesting topics for consideration, but his victim quickly catches up with him and jumps to his own false conclusions.

Having set the scene with generalities, Iago can then chip away with specifics; the cruel reminder that Desdemona behaved deceitfully when she married Othello, the painful reminder that Othello is an outsider (he does not appreciate the subtlety and worldliness of Venetian women), the alarming reminder that it was surprising for

CHECK THE FILM
The visual imagery of Parker's 1995 film links Iago very explicitly to the devil. He covers his hands in soot when he speaks of the 'Divinity of hell' (II.3.345), and is seen against a dark background, with a fire burning nearby, on several occasions.

**CHECK
THE BOOK**
For a psychoanalytic
reading of the play
that explores the
latent
homosexuality in
the text, see Andre
Green's essay in
John Drakakis (ed.),
*Shakespearean
Tragedy.*

Desdemona to choose Othello when there were other more 'natural' choices she could have made. From time to time Iago also reminds Othello that he loves and honours his 'free and noble nature' (line 203) and speaks only because he feels it is in his master's best interests. He continues the pretence that he is Cassio's trusted friend, which makes his reluctance to speak more plausible still. This scene suggests the power of silence, foreshadowing Iago's defiance at the end of the play. When he knows his poison has taken hold Iago is confident enough to make precise suggestions as to the course of action Othello should follow, leaving his victim alone in misery for a moment before returning to deal him further blows. After the exchanges between Othello and Desdemona and Emilia and Iago, the ensign is then able – because of his wife's unwitting assistance – to provide Othello with the evidence he desires so strongly. This is further proof of Iago's quick-witted opportunism. In this final part of the scene Iago adopts similar methods, initially reluctant to speak in specifics (Iago talks in generalities about honesty and the difficulty of obtaining proof) he then tells the false story of Cassio's lustful dream and asks a leading question about the handkerchief. Then, when Othello's thoughts turn to revenge, Iago knows it is time to revert to the role of loving and loyal assistant and friend. There is of course a horrible irony in the fact that by seeking to kill Cassio Othello is actually carrying out Iago's revenge for him. By the end of this scene Iago has achieved what he said he wanted in the first act: he is lieutenant.

How do we judge the noble Moor in Act III Scene 3? Essentially he is acted upon here, under pressure from the moment he enters. He is able to command his wife, although he seems uneasy during his conversation with her at the start of the scene. There is resignation in his line 'I will deny thee nothing' (line 76). We might feel that Othello is already on the brink of catastrophe, even before Iago's poison takes hold. As his wife leaves Othello utters these words:

> Excellent wretch! perdition catch my soul
> But I do love thee! and when I love thee not
> Chaos is come again.   (III.3.90–2)

These lines suggest that Othello will be utterly lost if his love is destroyed. Note the two negative abstract nouns that hint at the trouble to come: 'perdition' and 'Chaos'. The audience will be aware of the **dramatic irony** of these lines. So why, if he feels so strongly attached to Desdemona, does Othello give in to feelings of doubt and jealousy so very swiftly? Some commentators see these lines above as proof that the Moor is already in the grip of emotions that he cannot handle. Others point out that in spite of his other positive qualities and calm authority as a soldier, Othello is susceptible to jealousy. He is suggestible and insecure. This is not to underplay Iago's power in this scene. Othello has no reason to suspect his ensign of double dealing and as we have seen above, Iago has an enormous and subtle range of weapons in his armoury. Othello's brief interjections at lines 157 ('Zounds!') and 173 ('O misery!') suggest that the general cannot deal with the suggestions he is presented with. Note too that Othello is forced to ask a question and then respond to Iago's suggestions at lines 208 and 211. He is being prompted to think the worst. In this middle part of the scene Othello's utterances are short and uneasy, while Iago speaks at length, again suggesting the Moor's powerlessness in the face of vile insinuations.

Othello's decisiveness, which has stood him in good stead as a soldier, goes against him in this scene. He makes up his mind too quickly. Once he has made his mind up he refuses to look back, as he indicates himself at line 461. Left alone briefly he wonders wretchedly, 'Why did I marry?' suggesting that he has already decided that his wife is false. A few lines later he speaks of the 'curse of marriage' (line 272) – *his* Desdemona is gone forever, even though Othello continues to resist Iago's version of her until he is told the story of Cassio's dream. When he returns at line 332 there is a change in Othello. He speaks violently to Iago, 'Villain, be sure thou prove my love a whore' (line 362). Although Othello says he knows not what to believe ('I think my wife be honest, and think she is not', line 387), the violence of his speech and the images he conjures up indicate that Iago is winning. The opposition in the lines 387–90 comes almost at the middle of the play, perhaps suggesting that the general now has one of two opposing roads to take. Othello speaks of 'Poison, or fire, or suffocating streams'

> **CONTEXT**
>
> According to Aristotle, the tragic hero should not be entirely good or evil. Instead, he should possess a fatal flaw, which will incite pity and fear in the audience. Critics are divided about Othello. Some feel that he is flawless, while others think he is too easily moved to jealousy. What do you think?

(line 392), says his name is 'begrimed' (line 390) and then begins to curse, 'Death and damnation! O!' (line 399). At this point his speech begins to break down, signifying the disruption in his mind. Note too that he has started to use oaths – an example of the 'Iagoisation' of his speech that becomes more apparent as the play unfolds. This pattern continues later in the scene as Othello's words become more disjointed, his thoughts more wild and bloody (see lines 449–53 and 456–65). Othello's most arresting line is the ferocious, 'I'll tear her all to pieces' (line 434).

CHECK THE FILM

In Parker's film, Iago is driven by malice, but there is also a definite suggestion of homoerotic love. When Iago delivers the line 'I am your own forever' (III.3.482), he embraces Othello tightly, and tears appear in his eyes. In the final scene, Othello fatally wounds Iago, who crawls onto the bed to lie at his dead general's feet, where he expires.

We know there is no way back for him now; as he says himself, he is a resolute character and once he has decided on revenge his words are purposeful and ruthless (see lines 456–65, 472–6, 478–81). By this point in the scene Othello has regained some of his hold on himself, signified by the fact that he says more and initiates the plot to kill Cassio. But we know that he is fatally mistaken and can only fear the consequences of his resolution. It is also disquieting to note how Iago and Othello finish each other's lines at the end of the scene; further proof that the master is drawing horribly close to the evil servant and moving further away from his innocent wife. We might even argue that Iago has begun to replace Desdemona in Othello's affections, and that Iago's devotion must now be what Othello relies on instead of marital harmony. This is suggested by the serious oath taking at the end of the scene, when Othello says 'I greet thy love' (line 472) and Iago responds 'I am your own forever' (line 482).

GLOSSARY	
24	**a shrift** confessional
70	**mamm'ring** speaking hesitantly
126	**close delations** secret thoughts that are shut up inside
143	**leets and law-days** a leet was a local court of justice presided over by a magistrate
185	**exsufflicate** puffed up or fly-blown
203	**self-bounty** natural generosity
264	**aggard** a hawking term; wild, untameable
265	**jesses** straps on a hawk's legs, used to fasten the hawk to a leash on the falconer's wrist

269	**chamberers** gallant courtiers; seduction is implied
333	**mandragora** a soporific drug from the mandrake plant
349	**Pioneers** sappers or pioneers, the lowest rank of soldier
359	**Jove's dread clamours** thunder
390	**Dian** Diana, goddess of chastity
402	**bolster** share the same bed
406	**prime** lecherous, on heat
409	**imputation** opinion
453	**aspics' tongues** asps' tongues (an asp is a poisonous snake)
456	**Pontic sea** the Black Sea
459	**Propontic** Sea of Marmora, between the Black Sea and the Aegean
459	**Hellespont** Dardanelles Straits

CHECK THE FILM

Two recent versions of the play have suggested the poisoning of Othello's minds in different ways. Trevor Nunn (1990) has his Othello speak directly to camera, like Iago, when he starts doubting Desdemona's honesty. Oliver Parker (1995) includes a large number of close-ups of Othello's and Iago's heads in the same frame, and the pair look into each other's eyes frequently. The close-ups help to suggest the intimacy and intensity of the relationship in the second half of the play.

SCENE 4

- Othello is angry with Desdemona because he believes she has lost the handkerchief.

Desdemona asks the clown to inform Cassio that she has pleaded for him and hopes 'all will be well' (line 19). She then expresses her uneasiness about losing the handkerchief. There follows an awkward exchange with Othello, who finds it difficult to speak naturally and courteously to his wife. Desdemona returns to the subject of Cassio, but Othello ignores her remarks and asks her for the handkerchief. Desdemona replies that she does not have it with her. Othello stresses its importance, telling her that it has magical properties. He asks if it has been lost. Desdemona denies this and attempts to return once more to the subject of Cassio. Angered, Othello leaves. Emilia comments on his jealousy, while Desdemona again expresses her unhappiness at losing the handkerchief.

Iago and Cassio arrive together. Desdemona tells Cassio that he must be patient; Othello is out of humour. Iago enquires whether

CONTEXT

Critics have compared Othello to characters that appear in the Romance genre; his wooing of Desdemona with fantastic tales of his past and his travels suggest this. Shakespeare was to write several Romances at the end of his career: *Pericles, Cymbeline, The Winter's Tale* and *The Tempest.*

the general is angry and leaves, ostensibly with the intention of discovering the cause of Othello's anger. Desdemona tries to convince herself that it must be state matters that have disturbed her husband. She decides to look for Othello herself. She tells Cassio to wait behind. When she leaves Cassio's mistress Bianca enters. She is annoyed with her lover because he has not visited her recently. Cassio gives Bianca Desdemona's handkerchief, denying that it is a gift from 'a newer friend' (line 181). He castigates Bianca for her jealousy and says he found the handkerchief in his chamber. He then asks Bianca to leave, not wanting to be seen 'womaned' (line 194) if Othello returns. He agrees to visit Bianca soon.

COMMENTARY

This unhappy scene focuses on Desdemona. She is not only her husband's and Iago's victim; here she is also at the mercy of the clown, whose riddling shows how words can be misconstrued, mirroring the events of the previous scene. Emilia's function in this scene is to comment on what she sees and hears. She introduces the subject of Othello's jealousy, enabling us to appreciate just how much innocent faith Desdemona has in her husband. We quickly learn that we can rely on her judgement; Emilia rightly guesses that it is jealous thoughts which perturb Othello. Emilia is also wise in her definition of jealousy; 'It is a monster / Begot upon itself, born on itself' (lines 161–2). In succeeding scenes and acts we will see the aptness of these words. Shakespeare fills the scene with examples of alarming **dramatic irony**, for example Desdemona's words at lines 25–9 and 30–1. In spite of the fact that she lies to her husband about the loss of the handkerchief, we are likely to feel much sympathy for Desdemona. She does not appreciate the danger she is in, signified by her words at line 30 and is alarmed (rightly so, since his tone is hectoring) by her husband's description of the handkerchief and his repeated requests to see it. We can understand her falsehood; surely she is simply seeking not to anger Othello further? We will also feel sympathy for Desdemona as we listen to her excuse her husband's 'unkindness' in her speech at line 141. Having sympathised with Othello in the previous scene, we are likely to feel a little more critical of him here. We know that his suspicions are deeply painful to him, but his exchange with Desdemona does not show the Moor in a favourable light. The handkerchief is now

loaded with ominous significance; it seems to symbolise
Desdemona's honour. The mythic qualities that Othello endows it
with represent the Moor himself; its loss represents the 'break'
between the Moor and his wife. Desdemona is lost to Othello
because he has now adopted his ensign's view of the world. The
'magic in the web' (line 71) of the handkerchief represents the
'magic' of the Moor's union with the Venetian lady which has been
destroyed by Iago. Iago's triumph is driven home by his repetition
of the word 'angry' (lines 133, 135, 138); he has the power to control
the general's moods now. The exchange between Cassio and Bianca
shows us another example of a man speaking ungraciously to his
lover. We also see another example of amorous jealousy. Like
Desdemona, Bianca has to be satisfied with the treatment she
receives from her lover; she is powerless to change or direct him.

QUESTION

Do you agree with
critics who suggest
that Desdemona is
an assertive nag
when she pleads
for Cassio?

GLOSSARY

16 **catechize** teach by the catechism, by question and answer

26 **crusadoes** currency from Portugal, coins which were stamped with Christ's cross

72 **sibyl** prophetess

76 **mummy** a fluid derived from bodies that had been embalmed, used for magical or medicinal purposes

202 **be circumstanced** give in to circumstances or accept things the way they are

ACT IV

SCENE 1

- Overlooking a conversation, Othello sees Desdemona's handkerchief in Bianca's hand and believes that his wife has been unfaithful.
- Othello vows to murder Desdemona.
- Venetian visitors bring news that Othello has been recalled from Cyprus.

CHECK THE BOOK

For a discussion of the importance of the handkerchief and its qualities, see Robert B. Heilman's *Magic in the Web: Action and Language in 'Othello'.*

Iago continues to torture Othello with questions and crude images. He also torments him with allusions to the handkerchief. Iago again manipulates language expertly, forcing Othello to question him about his suspicions. When Iago suggests that he does not know for certain whether Cassio has lain 'With her, on her, what you will' (line 34) Othello becomes frenzied, falling down in a fit. While he is convulsed on the floor Iago gloats over him. Cassio enters and Iago immediately assumes the role of concerned and faithful servant. He sends Cassio away but tells him he needs to speak to him 'on great occasion' (line 58). When he comes round Othello agonises about being cuckolded. Iago tells Othello to withdraw so that he can overlook a conversation with Cassio, who, he says, has agreed to meet Desdemona secretly again. Othello falls in with this plan, which will, he hopes, provide him with the proof he longs for. When Othello withdraws Iago informs us that he will question Cassio about Bianca; Othello will believe that Cassio is speaking about Desdemona. Cassio returns and replies in a light-hearted way when Iago asks him about his intentions towards his mistress. Bianca comes in, still incensed about the handkerchief. She clings to her belief that it is 'some minx's token' (line 152). Othello seizes on this sighting of the handkerchief as proof that Desdemona has been unfaithful. When Cassio leaves to reason with Bianca, Othello emerges from his hiding place in a black mood. He is still torn between thoughts of his wife's sweetness and a desire to believe in her guilt. Iago ensures that vengefulness dominates. Othello decides to poison Desdemona that very night; Iago suggests that strangling her in the bed she has 'contaminated' (line 205) is more appropriate. The 'justice' (line 206) of this plan pleases Othello. Iago says that he will deal with the murder of Cassio himself and report back by midnight.

At this point Desdemona appears with Lodovico and other attendants. Othello has been recalled from Cyprus and Cassio is to be governor in his place. Desdemona welcomes this news. Othello presumes that she is glad because her lover has received promotion at his expense and strikes Desdemona, who leaves the stage. Lodovico is deeply shocked by what he has witnessed; he cannot believe that this is the 'noble Moor ... Whom passion could not shake?' (lines 264 and 266) After the general has left – almost incomprehensible in his rage – Iago tells Lodovico, with assumed reluctance, that Othello has been guilty of worse actions that striking his wife, ensuring that the Venetian visitors will view Othello darkly and believe that they have been deceived in him.

COMMENTARY

This opening scene of the fourth act is shocking and disturbing for a number of reasons. It is distressing to witness Othello spiralling downwards, signified by two examples of physical violence: his fit and the striking of Desdemona. The striking of Desdemona is particularly shocking, the more so because we know – and she says herself – that she does not deserve this humiliating (public) degradation. It is also chilling to watch Iago's icy enjoyment of his power as he watches the suffering Moor. His cool suggestion that Desdemona should be strangled is more horrifying still (as is Othello's concurrence with this plan). Why does Iago want Desdemona dead? This was not part of his original plan. It seems he has recognised that it is vital that she and Cassio die, before Othello decides to question them. In Act III Scene 3 Othello threatened Iago with death (**'woe upon thy life!'**, III.3.369) if he could not prove his wife a whore. He encourages Othello to strangle Desdemona because her death will help him to preserve his own life.

Iago commands Othello's imagination, conjuring up distressing images of infidelity early in the scene. He plays devil's advocate when he suggests that Desdemona's honour – like the handkerchief – is hers to give away as she chooses. We can see the devastating effect he has on Othello in the Moor's speech at line 35. Here Othello speaks disjointedly and distractedly – he is barely in control of his senses. His convulsion is the physical expression of his inner torment. It is horribly ironic that Iago calls his poisonous influence **'medicine'** at line 45. It also seems cruel that Iago should tell Othello to **'bear your fortune like a man'** (line 61), while simultaneously torturing him with thoughts of the 'millions' who make other men cuckolds every night. Iago knows that Othello's pride will render this idea unendurable. It is disconcerting to see the formerly noble Moor conceal himself so that he can eavesdrop. His vow to be **'most cunning in my patience'** (line 91) is both pitiful and alarming; Othello also intends to be 'most bloody' in the same line (we see how he is moving closer to the atrocity of the final act). We might also view his striking of Desdemona as a prelude to the physical violence that is to occur later in the play.

Cassio does not appear in a favourable light in his exchange with Iago. He seems rather heartless as he jokes about Bianca's fondness for him. But this exchange serves Shakespeare's – and Iago's – purposes admirably, as we see from Othello's first line when he emerges from his concealment: 'How shall I murder him, Iago?' he asks (line 167). It is in keeping with the events of this scene that the Moor should again ask Iago how to proceed; earlier we saw how he was reduced to asking questions rather than commanding. But we also sense Othello's helpless pain. Consider his exclamation at line 169: 'O Iago!' and the way in which the general is torn between thoughts of his wife's sweetness and her treachery; even now when he is under Iago's spell, we know how difficult it is for Othello to submit to the ensign's view (see lines 175–93). But he gives in, as his violent and shocking words at line 197 suggest: 'I will chop her into messes! Cuckold me!' Note the mixture of egotism and savagery here.

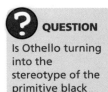

QUESTION

Is Othello turning into the stereotype of the primitive black man described in Act I Scene 1?

It is significant that this line and Othello's savage striking of Desdemona occur when Lodovico arrives in Cyprus. Lodovico represents the Venetian state and shows the civilised world's disturbed reaction to Othello's barbaric treatment of his wife. We see that Iago's influence has driven a wedge between husband and wife, and also between the general and his employers; Othello's star has fallen and he is becoming increasingly isolated by Iago and his jealousy.

GLOSSARY		
37	**fulsome**	nauseating, rank
40	**shadowing**	overspreading dark
76	**Confine yourself but in a patient list**	restrain yourself
87	**to cope**	to encounter or copulate with
102	**construe**	interpret
109	**caitiff**	wretch

121	**wit** judgement
145	**fitchew** polecat (this animal was thought to be lecherous and has a strong, musky smell. This a very derogatory way of referring to Bianca)
153	**hobby-horse** a loose woman

CHECK THE FILM

In Parker's 1995 film, Iago's control of Othello is demonstrated when the ensign locks his master behind bars. It is from this cell that Othello eavesdrops on Iago's conversation with Cassio. The camera occasionally offers the audience Othello's view of events, framed by the bars. We both see and sense his entrapment.

SCENE 2

- Othello confronts Desdemona, trying to get her to confess her guilt.
- Distraught and confused, Desdemona appeals to Iago for help.

Othello questions Emilia about his wife and Cassio. He is seeking to find further 'evidence' to add to the 'proof' of the handkerchief. Emilia insists that Desdemona is honest and chaste and warns Othello against jealousy. Othello asks Emilia to fetch his wife. She leaves the couple together. Othello now tries to elicit an admission of guilt from Desdemona, who courageously asserts her virtue. Overwrought, Othello weeps; Desdemona presumes that he is mourning her father, who has died. Othello then describes his mental suffering, employing an image of himself caught in everlasting shame. He also says that 'The fountain' (line 60) of his life has been polluted, becoming 'a cistern, for foul toads / To knot and gender in' (lines 62–3). Turning to his wife, Othello wonders how she can look so 'lovely fair' while being a 'weed' (line 68). Desdemona is bewildered by her husband's words; she asks what 'ignorant sin' she has committed (line 71). At this point Emilia returns. Believing that she is a 'simple bawd' (line 20) who has assisted Desdemona in her wantonness, Othello offers Emilia money and then leaves in disgust.

Emilia tries to comfort her mistress, who is miserable and bewildered. Desdemona asks Emilia to call Iago to her and also asks her to make her bed up with her wedding sheets. Emilia describes to her husband how Othello has 'bewhored' his wife (line 117) and

CONTEXT

The first stage Othello to physically strike his Desdemona was the nineteenth-century Italian actor, Tommaso Salvini.

Desdemona finally weeps. Iago assumes the role of gentle comforter while Emilia (ironically) waxes indignant; she believes that Desdemona has been slandered by some **'busy and insinuating rogue'** who has made Othello believe falsehoods (line 133). Desdemona asks Iago how she can win Othello back again. Iago tells her not to worry and to dry her tears. When Desdemona is summoned to supper by trumpets Roderigo appears; he has decided to return home, believing that Iago has deceived him with false hopes. Yet again Iago manages to talk him round, on this occasion persuading him to participate in the plot to murder Cassio. He says that his death is necessary so that Othello will be kept on in Cyprus as governor (Iago lies to Roderigo and tells him Othello is being sent to Mauritania).

COMMENTARY

This is another powerful and painful scene of misunderstandings. Emilia's remarks about trust in lines 12–19 do not touch Othello because he now misconstrues everything he hears and misreads what he sees (as in the previous scene). The tension within him and the struggle he is having in reconciling the warring emotions of love and jealousy, is dramatised through his use of contrasting images; the **'fountain'** (line 60) which becomes a **'cistern'** (line 62), he now looks **'grim as hell'** (line 65) when faced with the **'rose-lipped cherubin'** (line 64) Desdemona, who smells sweet but is now to him a **'weed'**. All of these images suggest how much under Iago's influence Othello is. His repetition of the words **'whore'** and **'strumpet'** throughout the scene indicates how far he is removed from the noble general of the first two acts, even if he still speaks poetically and with his customary measured tone at times (see lines 48–65). But his speech is infected by the imagery discussed above, even when he is eloquent and commanding. The insults he offers Desdemona and Emilia as he leaves make it hard to view Othello with much sympathy at this moment: his wife seems so helpless.

And yet sympathise we must. His wife's presence is painful to the Moor. When Desdemona defends herself he tries – rather weakly – to send her away. Whichever way she turns, Desdemona can find no relief; her husband's tone is by turns angry, pained and cold. As he leaves he speaks to her contemptuously, **'I cry you mercy then, / I** took you for that cunning whore of Venice / That married with Othello' (lines 90–2). Note the way in which Othello dramatises himself using the third person here; it is as if he has to distance himself from what he is saying to justify his words and actions. We will see this tendency again later in Act V.

Desdemona's innocent misery and lack of comprehension are indicated by the fact that she can barely bring herself to utter the word 'whore'. Note Desdemona's deep humility and generosity in this scene; she does not say that Othello was wrong to chide her (although she has bravely defended herself), just that he could have done it **'with gentle means'** (line 114). Desdemona also says earnestly that she still loves Othello dearly, and will continue to do so however unkindly he treats her. There is a good deal of pathos in her lines with Iago and Emilia, which contrast dramatically with Emilia's righteous, energetic and down to earth anger and Iago's pretended concern.

Dramatic irony plays its part here too. It is particularly ironic that Desdemona should seek help from the man who has effectively destroyed her, and ironic that Emilia should be so close to the truth when she describes the **'notorious knave'** (line 142) who has abused Othello, little knowing that her own husband is the very man. The lively prose exchange with Roderigo comes as something of a relief after the pain and harshness of the first two scenes of Act IV. It is difficult to feel much sympathy for Roderigo because he is so easily gulled and we will be dismayed to see how easily he is drawn into the plot against Cassio. But we must marvel at Iago, who has found someone to do the dirty work of killing for him – with very little effort. Note Iago's clinical, cold precision when describing **'the removing of Cassio'** (line 229). But he quickly resorts to the brutal, confident tone he usually adopts when discussing ideas with Roderigo; when his companion fails to understand him he says plainly that they must sort out the **'knocking out his brains'** (line 232).

QUESTION

Do you feel any pity for Othello in Act IV Scene 2, or is he simply a cruel bully?

GLOSSARY		
28	**procreants**	would be copulators
62	**cistern**	cesspool
		continued

QUESTION

Do you find the
end of this scene
comic or chilling?
Which lines could
be delivered with
humour?

123	**callat** slut
130	**Beshrew** curse, castigate
134	**cogging** cheating
134	**cozening** deceiving
177	**doff'st** put or fob off
190	**votarist** a nun
196	**fopped** fooled, duped
229	**determinate** effective, decisive

SCENE 3

- Desdemona is sent to prepare for bed.
- Unable to dismiss a melancholy song from her mind, she discusses female inconstancy with Emilia.

In contrast to the way in which her husband has spoken to her,
Lodovico politely wishes Desdemona goodnight and leaves to take
an evening walk with Othello. Othello speaks graciously enough to
Lodovico but then commands his wife to go to bed and dismisses
Emilia so that Desdemona is alone in her chamber. Emilia attempts
to comfort her mistress, saying she thinks that Othello 'looks
gentler than he did' (line 9). But she is puzzled and possibly alarmed
when she is told she is to be dismissed, saying stoutly that she
wished Desdemona had never met Othello. Desdemona says that
she still loves her husband, that even his bad moods 'have grace and
favour' in them (line 19). Ominously, she then tells Emilia that she
would like to be shrouded in her wedding sheets if she should die.
Desdemona narrates the sad story of one of her mother's maids
called Barbary, whose lover went mad and forsook her. Desdemona
says that she cannot get the song Barbary sang as she died out of her
mind. Emilia helps her mistress prepare for bed and the two women
briefly discuss Lodovico. Desdemona sings Barbary's willow song,
before returning to the topic of men. Desdemona cannot believe
that women can ever be unfaithful to their husbands; more

realistically, Emilia retorts that there are many who would betray their husbands. She then offers a realistic – if rather pessimistic – description of marriage. Desdemona ends the scene hoping that she will not behave badly when she is set a bad example, she will instead try to find a virtuous path to tread.

COMMENTARY

This is a melancholy and quiet scene which lacks some of the emotional 'fireworks' of the rest of Act IV. There is a terrible poignancy in almost every line that Desdemona utters and her 'willow' song mirrors her own sadness and points to her death. Like her husband, Desdemona also seems isolated, even though Emilia seeks to comfort her. The isolation comes because Desdemona insists on maintaining her good opinion of and love for her husband, while all around her doubt him. Emilia's dislike of Othello is very plain at line 16. Desdemona is also isolated in her idealistic, passive virtue, which is emphasised in this scene, preparing us for her submission in Act V. She seems most unworldly here, especially compared with the pragmatic Emilia. But this is appropriate; Shakespeare is emphasising Desdemona's innocence and the lost romance of her marriage; it is to her credit that Desdemona tries to keep this vision alive. Or is it? In this scene Desdemona is full of foreboding and seems to predict her own demise; she mentions winding sheets, her eyes itch, she is drawn to Barbary's melancholy song of death. Perhaps we are meant to believe that the heroine thinks that she can best please her husband by obeying his commands silently. Her obedience is further proof of her powerful love. But it is laced with delusion; she is perhaps foolish when she says even Othello's stubbornness pleases her. The willow song reinforces the melancholy atmosphere and prepares us for the tragic outcome; in the song the woman refuses to blame her lover and approves his scorn.

Note that Othello and Desdemona have been driven to tears in Act IV. And both wept – unwittingly – because of Iago's malignant influence. Othello has been in mourning for his marriage and his own and his wife's innocence. Desdemona has wept because she too has been unable to comprehend what is happening to her. The mind

CHECK THE BOOK

For comments about the female characters as victims, see Lisa Jardine's chapter on *Othello* in *Still Harping on Daughters*.

In the Elizabethan and Jacobean period, the wedding ring was a symbol not just of marriage, but also of the wife's chastity. What is the significance of the reference to 'a joint-ring' in this scene?

of the former has been destroyed; the body of the latter is shortly to be tortured, its life snuffed out.

GLOSSARY

10	**incontinent**	immediately
72	**a joint-ring**	a ring made of two separate parts
72	**lawn**	a fine linen fabric
73	**exhibition**	offer, allowance, gift

ACT V

SCENE 1

- Later that night Cassio is wounded by Roderigo, who is stabbed and killed by Iago.

As in the first scene of the play we are in a street at night, watching Iago issuing instructions to Roderigo. Iago informs us that he has two reasons for wanting Cassio murdered; firstly because he '**has a daily beauty in his life / That makes me ugly**' (lines 19–20) and secondly because Othello may '**unfold**' him to Cassio (line 21). When Roderigo conceals himself Iago tells us that it would be convenient for him if Cassio and Roderigo could manage to kill each other. When Cassio enters Roderigo lunges at him and receives a wound himself. Iago steps in and stabs Cassio in the leg. As he cries out for help, Othello appears. He mistakenly believes that Iago has murdered Cassio and determines to move on to his own act of vengeance.

Cassio's cries also draw Lodovico and Gratiano, who are nervous that they will be ambushed. Iago enters with a light and immediately attends on Cassio, calling the others over to help him. While they are preoccupied with Cassio, Iago takes his opportunity to stab Roderigo, who has also been calling for assistance. He then reassumes his role as valiant helper, binding Cassio's wound with his own shirt. Bianca has heard the fracas and is dismayed when she sees that Cassio has been hurt. As quick-witted as ever, Iago swiftly implicates her in the 'quarrel' between Cassio and Roderigo, whose body is discovered. The dead and wounded men are borne off. When Emilia arrives Iago informs her that Cassio's wounds are the 'fruit' of his 'whoring' (line 116) and continues to malign Bianca, who is taken away, in spite of the lack of evidence to suggest that she has done anything more villainous than dine with Cassio at her house. Emilia is dispatched to inform Othello and Desdemona of what has happened. Iago closes the scene with a tense aside; the dramatic and swift moving events of this night will either make or mar his fortunes forever.

COMMENTARY

In spite of his assurance and the ease with which he organises his cast of characters in this scene, Iago's final aside indicates the danger of his position. The urgency of these lines is in keeping with the swift and violent action of this scene; the brutality here also prepares us for the events of Act V Scene 2. Note the egotism of his words; Iago is wholly caught up with his own situation, while the audience is probably more concerned with Desdemona's fate. It might also be argued that Iago's closing lines can be delivered in an exultant tone: even at this critical moment the villain relishes his own evil.

With Roderigo out of the way, one potentially threatening voice has been silenced: but Cassio is still alive. Will he threaten Iago's security in the final scene? It is worth considering the ensign's new motive for killing Cassio; it seems that he cannot bear human virtue in any form. We have yet another example of Iago's evil opportunism in his bullying of Bianca, who becomes another convenient victim. In spite of his concern, we may feel that Iago still appears to be invincible; he has again gulled every character on stage.

Othello's brief appearance links him firmly with the atmosphere of dark treachery that prevails here; his ominous words remind us that there is worse to come. Ironically, it is another misunderstanding that spurs Othello on to his own act of violence: he believes Iago has killed Cassio. It is particularly horrible that Othello now seems

CHECK THE FILM
In Parker's 1995 film, Michael Maloney's Roderigo is seen suffering horribly after he is stabbed by Iago. He is gagging on his own blood as he dies. It is visually very clear that he is Iago's victim.

to act in direct response to the example he believes has been set by the devilish ensign. We are directed back to thoughts of Desdemona's plight right at the end of the scene when Emilia is sent to the citadel. The urgency with which she probably leaves the stage propels us into the final scene.

GLOSSARY

1	**bulk** stall, shop or a projected part of a building
11	**quat** boil or pimple
16	**bobbed** swindled
54	**spoiled** hurt, finished
78	**mangled** wounded

SCENE 2

- Othello smothers Desdemona in her bed.
- Iago's plots are uncovered.
- Realising his folly, Othello kills himself, leaving Iago to be punished by Cassio, who remains in Cyprus as governor.

QUESTION

In what ways do you find Act V Scene 2 an effective ending to the play as a tragedy?

Othello enters Desdemona's bed chamber carrying a lantern. In a long speech he outlines his thoughts; he intends to kill his wife, but not to shed her blood. He sees himself as a just revenger, who is preventing Desdemona from betraying more men. At the same time he is struck by the enormity of the violent act he is about to commit; even now he regrets his intentions: he knows that he will not be able to bring Desdemona back to life after he has killed her. Othello kisses his sleeping wife, whose physical beauty still has a powerful effect on him, swaying him momentarily from his purpose. Yet again he is drawn to kiss her and weep; but he insists his tears must be cruel tears. Desdemona wakes up. Othello speaks to her calmly, asking her if she has prayed. He does not want to murder her 'unprepared spirit' (line 31). Desdemona is scared by her husband's words and looks and begs to know what disturbs

Othello. Othello returns to the topic of the handkerchief, which Desdemona denies giving to Cassio. She weeps when she learns that Cassio is (as Othello believes) dead, realising finally that she is 'undone' (line 75). Othello believes she is weeping because she mourns Cassio and becomes angry. He stifles Desdemona. Meanwhile Emilia is knocking on the door. Othello ignores her calls until he believes his wife is no longer breathing. When he discovers that Cassio has not been killed Othello is perturbed. Desdemona revives and calls out, reasserting her innocence. Emilia's attention turns immediately to her mistress and she demands to know who has killed her. Desdemona's reply is characteristically generous; she assumes responsibility for her own death and asks to be commended to her husband. Othello briefly pretends that he did not kill his wife, but then admits his guilt. Emilia turns on him. Othello relates the story of his wife's unfaithfulness (as he believes it) and tells Emilia that it was her husband Iago who told him Desdemona was false. Shocked, Emilia continues to insult Othello. She then shouts for help and Montano, Gratiano and Iago rush in. Emilia confronts Iago and he admits that he told Othello Desdemona was false, but then warns her to hold her tongue. But Emilia will not be silenced. She continues to lament her mistress's death loudly and explains how the handkerchief came to be in Iago's possession. Othello finally understands the truth and tries to strike Iago, who escapes, after stabbing his wife. Othello is disarmed, guards are sent after Iago, and Emilia asks to be placed on the bed so that she be near her mistress. Emilia dies, reiterating Desdemona's innocence. Overcome by despair, Othello now begins to think of his own death. He feels both helpless ('Who can control his fate?', line 263) and determined to be punished ('Whip me, ye devils', line 275). He cannot bear the pain of losing Desdemona.

Iago is escorted back on to the stage by guards. Lodovico and Montano accompany him and Cassio is carried on in a chair. The characters who remain are now gathered to witness Othello's wounding of 'honest' Iago and the general's own death. Othello hopes to kill Iago when he strikes him, but then says he is glad that his foe has survived; death represents happiness to him. When he is asked why he has behaved so villainously, Iago takes refuge in silence. However, his plots against Cassio are discovered (letters

CHECK THE BOOK
For a discussion of Iago as an example of supreme, satanic evil, see A. C. Bradley's *Shakespearean Tragedy*.

found in the dead Roderigo's pocket reveal all.) The disgraced lieutenant confirms that he found the handkerchief in his chamber, and that Iago has admitted that he placed it there. Othello now feels the full weight of his crime and calls out in agony 'O fool, fool, fool!' (line 321). Lodovico promises that Iago will be tortured and then informs Othello he will be held prisoner too, until the Venetian senate has decided his fate. But Othello will not be humiliated in this way. He reminds his listeners of the services he has done the state and asks to be remembered as one 'that loved not wisely, but too well; / Of one not easily jealous, but, being wrought, / Perplexed in the extreme' (lines 342–4). Condemning himself for his actions he then kills himself with his sword, falling on the bed as he dies. Lodovico curses Iago, who is left to Cassio's mercy as governor of Cyprus. Othello's fortune is passed on to Gratiano. Lodovico says he will return to inform the Venetian senate of the terrible events that have occurred.

COMMENTARY

The stillness of the opening of this final scene contrasts dramatically with the events and mood of the previous scene; and the long section in which Othello stands over and then smothers Desdemona seems to suggest that time is finally moving more slowly (and as a result, agonisingly). Othello's opening speech reveals a number of things. Firstly, that the tragic hero sees himself as an agent of justice, whose purpose is to prevent Desdemona from committing further sins. Later in the scene he tells us that he views her death as a sacrifice, not a murder (as if he were a priest engaged in a religious ritual – note the sense of detachment and righteousness). But perhaps he protests too much. The repetition of 'it is the cause' (line 1), combined with the fact that Othello still cannot bring himself to name the cause, indicates that even now the tragic protagonist finds it impossible to tear himself away from his wife by killing her. We might also feel that the litany of 'it is the cause' should be read as self-justification. Othello's desire to avoid spilling Desdemona's blood is significant. Some critics suggest that this means he seeks to avoid the marks of murder and thus attempts to avoid blame and guilt. Others might see a desire to leave Desdemona as she is – Othello speaks about her white skin, which is as 'smooth, as monumental alabaster' (line 5). It is as if he really wants her to live, or at least, not to look as if she is dead. However, the reference to alabaster calls to mind a tomb: in Othello's mind his wife is dead already. The complexity of these lines and images is continued through the other imagery that Othello uses in his opening speech. He speaks of a rose withering on a tree, and then says '**Be thus when thou art dead and I will kill thee / And love thee after**' (lines 18–19); note the force of the middle phrase here ('and I *will* kill thee'): the modal verb suggests determination. But there are pain and reluctance here too. Othello has to use symbols: Desdemona is a rose, he is acting for Justice. By symbolising his wife he again avoids confronting his deed head on, as he did when he refused to name the 'cause' (reason) for his jealousy and the murder. The opposition in Othello is summed up by his lines about weeping and sorrow, which is '**heavenly**' (line 21), the opposite of what sorrow should be. Othello believes he is acting out of love. All the images in these lines portray the sorrow he feels and the enormity of his deed. It is important to remember that Othello is immeasurably calm at this point. He does not speak passionately or rashly; he measures his words and seems in control of his faculties, although the imagery of opposition suggests that he is still torn mentally; he is both in control and confused.

Othello's terrible control is shown when Desdemona wakes up. Agonisingly, he is made to say that he will kill Desdemona several times before he actually smothers her. Her pleading is deeply distressing. At the moment that he kills her Othello is still obsessed by the handkerchief, and uses Iago's coarse language, suggesting that we are not perhaps to view him as the sole perpetrator of this crime. Othello seems to revert to mercy almost as soon as he has smothered his wife; he does not want her to linger in pain. This adds to the pathos of Desdemona's demise, which is heightened when she murmurs to Emilia that Othello is not to blame for her death. There is a low point for the hero when he tries to think of a way of concealing the murder at line 94, and again when he tells Emilia that he did not kill Desdemona. Perhaps Shakespeare is trying to show Othello's confusion; his speech at line 90 is a little disjointed, with short phrases and questions. It is completed by a yelp of pain, '**My**

QUESTION

To what extent is Iago responsible for Desdemona's death?

wife, my wife, what wife? I have no wife; / O, insupportable! O heavy hour!' (lines 96–7). Admittedly Othello does not confess his own guilt or express remorse here, but he clearly understands what he has lost. That he sees Desdemona's death as a monumental loss can be confirmed by the fact that he thinks there should now be 'a huge eclipse / Of sun and moon, and that th'affrighted globe / Should Yawn at alteration' (lines 97–9). He feels that nature should reflect the chaos he finds himself mired in.

Emilia becomes the voice of the audience in this scene; we must have an outlet for our feelings of outrage. The repetition of 'my husband' (lines 138, 142, 145) is highly charged; Emilia is as reluctant as Desdemona to believe her husband is not what he seems. Her outpourings serve two functions; she mourns Desdemona and offers a tribute to her mistress's virtues, while also reconfirming the strength of the love she felt for Othello. Emilia is the guardian of Desdemona's honour, a role Othello should have assumed. Emilia's castigation of Othello reminds us how far the noble Moor has fallen and the cruelty of her words might perhaps represent some kind of poetic justice. Othello recognises the justice of Emilia's description when he reiterates her words, 'O fool, fool, fool!' Othello redeems himself further when he asks plaintively, 'why should honour outlive honesty?' (line 243). But does Othello remain somewhat deluded and self-dramatising, as some critics have suggested? He still insists that he is honourable: has his pride been his downfall? In his final speech the Moor presents himself as both hero and villain. He reminds Lodovico and the others (with characteristic self-effacement) that he has been of service to the Venetian state, and seems to want to insist on his identity as heroic soldier, not disastrous husband. But we must remember that Othello also recognises that he deserves to be tortured and to die. Othello is preoccupied with himself but at the same time he focuses sharply on Desdemona, killing himself 'to die upon a kiss' (line 357). Consider how accurate Othello's final assessment of himself is: did he give in to jealousy too easily? Was he perplexed in the extreme? Did he love unwisely?

CONTEXT

Dr Johnson found Act V Scene 2 so moving as to be unendurable.

Iago says less in this scene than in any other scene in the play; and in some ways his silence is as powerful as his speech. Has he been defeated? We might feel that he is not diminished by the revelation of his crimes: is Iago gloating when he says to Othello, 'I bleed, sir, but not killed' (line 285). His last line can certainly seem defiant. Many critics feel that the ensign remains an enigma. However, his devilment is clearly recognised by all the characters on stage. Iago's final acts are brutal and unnatural. There is a troubling irony in the fact that his last crime mirrors Othello's: he too kills his honest wife to preserve his honour. The closeness of Iago and Othello also seems to be suggested by the references to unchristian behaviour. Iago is a 'cursed slave' (line 289), a 'demi-devil' (line 298); Othello is responsible for a 'monstrous' (line 186) murder and then destroys himself in an act of heathenish self-slaughter. However, our final responses to Othello and Iago will be very different; we will feel the great tragedy of the Moor's death and relieved and glad that his tormentor will be tortured.

QUESTION

How does Othello's final speech sum up the nature of his downfall?

GLOSSARY		
12	**Promethean heat**	in Greek mythology Prometheus brought life-giving fire to men from Heaven
13	**relume**	light again
141	**chrysolite**	topaz
159	**gull**	dupe
245	**the swan**	it was believed that swans sang before they died
251	**the ice-brook's temper**	a fine Spanish sword, a sword tempered by plunging it into icy water
265	**butt**	target
266	**sea-mark**	beacon or landmark to sail by
283	**I look down towards his feet**	an allusion to the idea that the Devil had cloven hoofs

EXTENDED COMMENTARIES

TEXT 1 - I.1.81–138

This exchange occurs immediately after Iago has informed Roderigo that he hates Othello, and follows him only to 'serve my turn upon him' (I.1.42).

> BRABANTIO [*appears above*] *at window*
> BRABANTIO: What is the reason of this terrible summons?
> What is the matter there?
> RODERIGO: Signior, is all your family within?
> IAGO: Are your doors locked?
> BRABANTIO: Why? Wherefore ask you this?
> IAGO: Zounds, sir, you're robbed, for shame put on your gown! 85
> Your heart is burst, you have lost half your soul,
> Even now, now, very now, an old black ram
> Is tupping your white ewe! Arise, arise,
> Awake the snorting citizens with the bell
> Or else the devil will make a grandsire of you,   90
> Arise I say!
> BRABANTIO: What, have you lost your wits?
> RODERIGO: Most reverend signior, do you know my voice?
> BRABANTIO: Not I, what are you?
> RODERIGO: My name is Roderigo.
> BRABANTIO: The worser welcome!
> I have charged thee not to haunt about my doors: 95
> In honest plainness thou hast heard me say
> My daughter is not for thee; and now in madness,
> Being full of supper and distempering draughts,
> Upon malicious bravery dost thou come
> To start my quiet?   100
> RODERIGO: Sir, sir, sir –
> BRABANTIO: But thou must needs be sure
> My spirit and my place have in them power
> To make this bitter to thee.
> RODERIGO: Patience, good sir!
> BRABANTIO: What tell'st thou me of robbing? This is Venice:
> My house is not a grange.

CONTEXT

Christian traditions of the Renaissance suggested that Africans were descendants of Noah's son Ham, who was cursed by his father. Thus, it held that they were an accursed race.

RODERIGO: Most grave Brabantio,   105
In simple and pure soul I come to you –
IAGO: Zounds, sir, you are one of those that will not
serve God, if the devil bid you. Because we come to
do you service, and you think we are ruffians, you'll
have your daughter covered with a Barbary horse;   110
you'll have your nephews neigh to you, you'll have
coursers for cousins and jennets for germans!
BRABANTIO: What profane wretch art thou?
IAGO: I am one, sir, that comes to tell you your daughter
and the Moor, are now making the beast with two backs.   115
BRABANTIO: Thou art a villain!
IAGO: You are a senator!
BRABANTIO: This thou shalt answer. I know thee, Roderigo!
RODERIGO: Sir, I will answer anything. But I beseech you,
If't be your pleasure and most wise consent,
As partly I find it is, that your fair daughter   120
At this odd-even and dull watch o' th' night,
Transported with no worse nor better guard
But with a knave of common hire, a gondolier,
To the gross clasps of a lascivious Moor –
If this be known to you, and your allowance,   125
We then have done you bold and saucy wrongs.
But if you know not this, my manners tell me
We have your wrong rebuke. Do not believe
That from the sense of all civility
I thus would play and trifle with your reverence   130
Your daughter, if you have not given her leave,
I say again, hath made a gross revolt,
Tying her duty, beauty, wit and fortunes
In an extravagant and wheeling stranger
Of here, and everywhere. Straight satisfy yourself: 135
If she be in her chamber or your house
Let loose on me the justice of the state
For thus deluding you.
BRABANTIO: Strike on the tinder, ho!

CHECK THE NET
For a biography of Shakespeare, some general advice on studying Shakespeare, and some specific comments on *Othello* see **www.bbc.co.uk/learning**.

This is not the first example of Iago's sure footed manipulation of events and the perceptions of others in *Othello*. Although this is the very first scene and only 80 lines in, the ensign has already succeeded in colouring Roderigo's view of Othello's marriage in order to obtain his assistance to 'Call up her [Desdemona's] father, / Rouse him, make after him, poison his delight' (I.1.66–7). This exchange is the result of Iago's plan to 'Plague him [Brabantio] with flies' (I.1.70). Iago's use of metaphors is typical of the ensign, who is associated with images of poison, corruption and disease throughout the play. In Act I Scene 1 Shakespeare starts to prepare us for the poisoning of Othello's mind which occurs in Act III.

> **CONTEXT**
>
> Cyprus was one of Venice's colonies, from 1489–1571. *Othello* is set in 1570–71, making the hero one of the last men sent to defend the island from the Turks.

The location of this scene is significant, and ties in with the imagery that Iago and Roderigo use. It is night-time, and the two levels of the stage used (Brabantio at the window, Iago and Roderigo concealed in the darkness of the street below) signifies the disruption that they have come to inform Brabantio of. There is a sense in which Brabantio's physical security (his house) is threatened along with his peace of mind. Iago refers to Desdemona's elopement using a verb that signifies an assault on Brabantio's property; the old man has been 'robb'd'. Roderigo's descriptions of Desdemona's movements also add to the atmosphere of disruption and disorder, and establish the danger of the Venice at night; 'At this odd-even and dull watch o' the night' Brabantio's daughter has been transported to the 'gross clasps of a lascivious Moor' by 'a knave of common hire, a gondolier'. The different tones and roles of the characters in this scene also convey disruption. Brabantio begins the scene assuming the role of angry and confident patriarch. We know he is powerful man because he speaks of 'my spirit and my place' and his property (and not just his house; when he says 'my daughter is not for thee' to Roderigo we know that Brabantio also looks upon his offspring as a possession. This idea follows on neatly from the earlier use of 'robbed'). He dismisses Roderigo in a commanding tone at line 95 and is offended by Iago's presence too; in particular he finds the ensign's mode of address offensive; 'What profane wretch art thou?' he enquires disdainfully before insulting Iago as a 'villain'. Brabantio's social position is undermined in this scene, not just by the 'wheeling stranger' who has eloped with his daughter, but also by Iago's saucy words and Roderigo's description of the 'gross revolt'. We know that the prosperous father's authority is subverted too because his utterances contain questions as well as threats, and his final line in this exchange suggests alarm. Instead of directing his social inferiors, Brabantio finds himself acting in response to them.

Roderigo follows Iago's instructions in this exchange. He speaks politely to Brabantio, reinforcing our sense of the father's important social position. The terms in which Roderigo describes Desdemona's elopement, and in particular Othello echo the descriptions of the Moor offered earlier in the scene. The images he employs are negative, focusing on the unnatural quality of the match and Desdemona's disobedience. This marriage is a subversion of the natural order; Desdemona has 'made a gross revolt'. Roderigo is a representative of Venetian society, one of the 'curled darlings' (I.2.68) Desdemona has rejected and his xenophobic view of her marriage is one that Brabantio can understand; as we see later in the first act, he too views his daughter's marriage as an incomprehensible rejection of everything she has known. Note the social snobbery of Roderigo's descriptions, which is accentuated by his rather exaggerated mode of speaking. Brabantio and Roderigo speak the same language of power, which proves to be impotent in this scene. We already know Roderigo is a failed suitor, and now Brabantio's authority is denied.

Iago speaks a different language entirely, and although he does not have the long speeches in this exchange and is rejected by Brabantio, we can see his emerging power. His racist descriptions of Othello are not so far removed from Roderigo' term 'lascivious Moor', which is also part of the black stereotype that is being created. But his imagery is far more crude than either of the other two gentlemen's speech. His references to 'an old black ram', 'a Barbary horse' and 'the beast with two backs' reinforce the idea that Desdemona has made an unnatural match and cast Othello in a repugnant role: he is an animal, specifically a sexual animal. Race and sex are clearly going to be important issues in *Othello*. Iago's reduction of the Desdemona–Othello match to bestial sexuality is typical of the ensign, who is associated with unpleasant animal imagery throughout the play. We might feel that the images here tell us more about Iago's character than Othello's because we are already aware of the ensign's hatred; earlier in the scene he told us

> **CONTEXT**
>
> In spite of the fact that *Othello* is set in Venice, Iago is a shortened form of the Spanish name Santiago, or, in English, St James. St James of Spain was known as 'St James the Moor-killer' because of his campaigns against the Moors. Roderigo is also a Spanish name.

CHECK THE BOOK

For a discussion about the way Shakespeare portrays race in the play, see Barbara Everett, '"Spanish" Othello: The Making of Shakespeare's Moor', *Shakespeare Survey 35* (1982), pp. 101–12.

that he wishes to revenge himself on the Moor. We know that Iago is an untrustworthy villain. But we also see that Iago is persuasive and self-confident. He answers Brabantio back and forces his own interpretation of events on him too. Some would argue that Iago's plain and pithy interjections really capture the angry father's attention in this scene. Roderigo receives threats and finds it difficult to assert himself sufficiently to elaborate on his tale, but after Iago's speech at line 107 the senator seems to begin to take note. We might also feel that the imagery that Roderigo uses to describe Othello has come straight out of Iago's mouth and simply reiterates what the ensign has already said in his own vulgar way. Gradually we realise that Iago enjoys manipulating language. We also come to understand that the ensign is associated with lust not love; a key idea that is developed later in the play. This extract reveals Iago's ability to improvise: he sets the pace and controls the drama. It was his idea to wake Brabantio up and here he gets the result he wanted, an angry father.

This is an exchange of contrasts and discord which sets the scene for the events that follow. The contrasts are reflected in the imagery and setting, which establish a number of themes and ideas that are going to be important in *Othello*: social disruption, class and power, delusion and knowledge, male and female sexuality and black and white. The rather chaotic feel signifies that disruption has already occurred and we know that Othello and Desdemona's marriage is going to be the focal point for future disruption because these three characters react to it so strongly and describe it in such negative terms. Contrasts exist between the characters and their language, and we are also aware of the difference between Desdemona and her husband; she is the 'white ewe' while he is the 'black ram'. She has been stolen, but we also know she has given herself away because she has chosen to elope secretly. We have Venice, a civilised place associated with power, prosperity and order has been assaulted by a 'wheeling stranger'. The urgency and initial confusion of the discussion here underlines the idea that this play is going to focus on conflict and dislocation of some kind, centring on this stranger. We now wonder how the tension that has been set up in this scene will be resolved; particularly the evident dislike and disdain these three characters feel for Othello. We can see that the villain of the piece has already had some success in getting his view of the Moor accepted; now we want to see this character for ourselves.

TEXT 2 - II.1.138–99

Recently arrived in Cyprus, Desdemona anxiously awaits Othello's arrival, passing the time by sparring with Iago.

DESDEMONA: These are old fond paradoxes to make
fools laugh i'the alehouse. What miserable praise hast
thou for her that's foul and foolish?   140
IAGO: There's none so foul, and foolish thereunto,
But does foul pranks which fair and wise ones do.
DESDEMONA: O heavy ignorance, thou praisest the worst
best. But what praise couldst thou bestow on a
deserving woman indeed? One that in the authority   145
of her merit did justly put on the vouch of very
malice itself?
IAGO: She that was ever fair and never proud,
Had tongue at will, and yet was never loud,
Never lacked gold, and yet went never gay,   150
Fled from her wish, and yet said 'now I may',
She that, being angered, her revenge being nigh,
Bade her wrong stay, and her displeasure fly,
She that in wisdom never was so frail
To change the cod's head for the salmon's tail,   155
She that could think, and ne'er disclose her mind,
See suitors following, and not look behind,
She was a wight, if ever such wights were –
DESDEMONA: To do what?
IAGO: To suckle fools, and chronicle small beer.   160
DESDEMONA: O, most lame and impotent conclusion!
Do not learn of him, Emilia, though he be thy
husband. How say you, Cassio, is he not a most
profane and liberal counsellor?
CASSIO: He speaks home, madam, you may relish him   165
more in the soldier than in the scholar.
IAGO: [aside] He takes her by the palm; ay, well said,
whisper. With as little a web as this will I ensnare as
great a fly as Cassio. Ay, smile upon her, do: I will

CONTEXT

Othello (1603) was written during Shakespeare's great tragic period; *Hamlet* preceded *Othello* in 1600, and *King Lear* and *Macbeth* were first performed in 1604–6.

---

gyve thee in thine own courtesies. You say true, 'tis   170
so in-deed. If such tricks as these strip you out of
your lieutenantry, it had been better you had not
kissed your three fingers so oft, which now again you
are most apt to play the sir in. Very good, well kissed,
and excellent courtesy: 'tis so indeed! Yet again, your   175
fingers to your lips? would they were clyster-pipes
for your sake! (*Trumpets within*)
The Moor! I know his trumpet!
CASSIO: 'Tis truly so.
DESDEMONA: Let's meet him and receive him.
Enter othello *and Attendants.*
CASSIO: Lo, where he comes!
OTHELLO: O my fair warrior!
DESDEMONA: My dear Othello!   180
OTHELLO:
It gives me wonder great as my content
To see you here before me! O my soul's joy,
If after every tempest come such calms
May the winds blow till they have wakened death,
And let the labouring bark climb hills of seas,   185
Olympus-high, and duck again as low
As hell's from heaven. If it were now to die
'Twere now to be most happy, for I fear
My soul hath her content so absolute
That not another comfort like to this   190
Succeeds in unknown fate.
DESDEMONA: The heavens forbid
But that our loves and comforts should increase
Even as our days do grow.
OTHELLO: Amento that, sweet powers!
I cannot speak enough of this content,
It stops me here, it is too much of joy.   195
And this, and this the greatest discords be   *They kiss.*
That e'er our hearts shall make.
IAGO: [*aside*]
O, you are well tun'd now: but I'll set down
The pegs that make this music, as honest
As I am.

CHECK THE FILM

In the 1995 film, the director, Parker, chooses to show us the consummation of Othello and Desdemona's marriage. The couple's mutual sexual pleasure is apparent. They are physically 'well tun'd' (II.1.198). Parker also includes sexual scenes that reflect Othello's paranoia. In particular, there is a sequence of rapidly cut shots of Desdemona in bed with Cassio, which conveys Othello's jealousy very clearly. We can see, as well as hear, what obsesses the hero.

Like so many others in *Othello*, this extract is laced with **dramatic irony** and tension. The reunion between Othello and Desdemona should be a moment of great happiness, but the audience is unable to share in their delight because of Iago's presence. His calculating, crude asides taint and undermine the joy of this meeting. As usual, Iago is acting a role, although the sentiments he expresses in this scene are – ironically – close to the opinions about women that he proffers in his soliloquies throughout the play and in Act V Scene 2 when he is unmasked. Is Iago so clever, so in control, that he can even get away with pretending to pretend? Desdemona and Cassio, who are taken in by the blunt soldier act, do not really take Iago seriously in this scene, so far as they are concerned he is an amusement. The audience knows better. Iago alarms rather than entertains us. We realise that he should be feared. His asides in this scene provide a running commentary; through them we are able to observe the progress of Iago's plots and his impressive improvisational ability. The imagery he uses in his asides reinforces our fears and also helps to establish Iago's deadly power. He speaks gleefully of spinning a 'web' to 'ensnare as great a fly as Cassio'. It is ironic that Cassio has spoken contemptuously towards Iago at line 165, now in an aside we see that it is the social and professional inferior who really has the power; Iago intends to use Cassio's superior social skills and sophistication against him.

CHECK THE NET
For historical context and summaries see **www.campusnut. com**.

He will also of course succeed in misconstruing the open, playful sexuality that Desdemona displays in this scene when she says to Emilia, 'O most lame and impotent conclusion:'. Some critics are uncomfortable with Desdemona's participation in this bawdy exchange, but Shakespeare deliberately stresses her sexuality here and on other occasions for several important reasons. Firstly, Desdemona's genuine physical attraction to Othello helps to establish the hero's innocence of witchcraft, and aids our reception of the couple as a good match; it is important that we understand how – as Iago puts it – 'well tun'd' Desdemona and Othello are. This makes the collapse of their marriage truly tragic and affecting. Desdemona's sexuality is also important to the plot. Iago's evil designs rely on Desdemona's sexual attractiveness; in order to make Othello believe that his wife has committed adultery, the heroine must be a sexual creature. Her confidence and wit, shown in

Desdemona's direct, playful questions at lines 139 and 159, are an important part of her appeal too. These qualities will also be used against the heroine. Later in the play Iago succeeds in making Desdemona's speech seem unreliable. There is a cruel irony in the fact that Desdemona warns Emilia playfully about believing what her husband says; it is she who needs to beware of Iago's words and opinions. It is also ironic that Iago's description of 'a deserving woman' (lines 148–58) comes to suit Desdemona perfectly in Acts IV and V, when the heroine displays a submissive character and refuses to condemn her husband even after he has smothered her.

Although the other characters do not take Iago's misogyny seriously, we do. As Iago's plots progress it becomes clear that his plans rely heavily on the heartless manipulation of Desdemona, Emilia and Bianca. He also influences the way in which the other male characters think of and respond to these women. He changes Roderigo from a love-lorn suitor into a lustful would-be murderer; Cassio treats and speaks of his mistress with contempt when he is under Iago's influence, and of course, Othello becomes the 'cruel Moor' (V.2.247) under his tutelage, physical and verbal abuser of women. But the audience is already likely to question what the ensign says about the female sex. Although she has disobeyed her father, Desdemona displays none of the negative traits Iago describes in this scene, and as the drama unfolds, we realise that women are victims rather than fools in *Othello*. Interestingly, this exchange also contains irony that eventually works against Iago. The ensign says that he can only stand a quiet woman ('never loud'), who will 'ne'er disclose her mind'. At the end of the play Iago's villainy is revealed when Emilia refuses to be silent and discloses her thoughts extremely freely. Iago does not simply have a low opinion of women: he also wants to degrade them. This emerges more fully in his soliloquy at line 284 in this scene, but we get a hint of it here. His reference to 'clyster-pipes' (a syringe for a vaginal douche) at line 176 is extremely crude. Throughout *Othello* Iago employs similar vulgar and degrading images to describe female sexuality, which are devastatingly effective. We know from his earlier descriptions of Desdemona as a 'land carrack' (I.2.50) and his saucy chat with Cassio in Act II Scene 3 – when he describes her as being 'full of game' (II.3.19), 'sport for Jove' (II.3.17) and having an eye

QUESTION

Does this scene alter your opinion of Desdemona? Why do you think her 'playful' exchanges with Iago have been omitted from some productions?

which 'sounds a parley of provocation' (II.3.21–2) – that he cannot think of the heroine as possessing any real worth. He has to belittle her. Desdemona's love for the Moor is so inexplicable to Iago that he has to describe it as lust. This unpleasant reference to clyster pipes also suggests the ensign's urge to reduce everything to his own base level.

However, although we want to repulse Iago and repudiate all his utterances in this scene, the villain keeps drawing us back to him. He butts in, whispers, invites us to collude with him and view what he is observing through his eyes. We don't hear what Desdemona and Cassio say at line 167, so we are compelled to listen to Iago's interpretation of their conversation; this is precisely what the ensign does to all the other characters in this play; he forces them to accept his version of events. It is a measure of Iago's might that he is even able to undermine what is a powerful and loving reunion.

Let us consider this reunion closely. Othello and Desdemona's kisses suggest the erotic strength of their love. We know just how powerful Othello's emotions are because his first thought in this scene is for his 'fair warrior' (note the convergence of soldier and lover implied by the hero's opening words). Look at the positivity of his greeting: it gives Othello 'wonder great as my content / To see you here before me'; Desdemona is his 'soul's joy'. This greeting is an eloquent expression of Othello's love and the delight he feels in his marriage. It is deeply moving. However, even before Iago offers us his snide and threatening aside of lines 197–9, we are aware that there is a worrying undercurrent. Othello says – innocently – 'I fear / My soul hath her content so absolute / That not another comfort like to this / Succeeds in unknown fate'. There is a horrible irony here. Othello thinks that he is at the apogee of happiness; we know that an 'unknown fate' does indeed await him, but it is not a comforting one. Note the uncomprehending negativity of Othello's words: in his next speech he says that he feels too content, 'it is too much joy'. We might feel that this negativity, which Desdemona rejects, hints at the tragedy to come and also undermines the power of the kisses that follow these lines. We never see Othello and Desdemona kiss again until the final scene when kissing becomes the prelude to killing. It is almost as if Othello's first speech to

CHECK THE FILM

In the 1990 TV film it is clear that Othello idealises Desdemona, and puts her on a pedestal. When he arrives in Cyprus, he lifts her up and places her on top of an upturned case that is being used as a platform. Desdemona seems to tower over her husband, who gazes up at her admiringly. The camera moves around and we see from Desdemona's point of view, as the young bride looks down at Othello. The camera angle clearly suggests that Othello has been disorientated by love, and that he has lost some of his power.

QUESTION

Consider all the possible meanings of 'well tun'd'.

Desdemona here signifies the peak of their marriage, while his second speech suggests that they are on the downward slope already, even though, as Iago says they seem to be 'well tun'd'. Othello's amen is interesting. The fact that Othello feels they need a prayer might be considered alarming, even though it suggests his compatibility with Desdemona and her point of view. The sea metaphor Othello employs to describe the happiness he feels at lines 183–7 is also important. Here the general seems to suggest that he would be prepared to come through dangers of the worst kind so long as he had Desdemona to greet him at the other end. There is irony and pathos in this image. It does convey the strength and depth of Othello's love, but his faith is alarming because we know that Iago is preparing to destroy the calm. We wonder how Othello will rise to the challenge of a battle in his personal life because we know he is already overwhelmed by his feelings for Desdemona. Thus even Othello's joy seems to add to the tension and sense of foreboding.

This scene is important because it is a turning point. It is appropriate that it occurs at the harbour in Cyprus, suggesting a new focus and new influences. All the characters behave and speak in ways which are typical of them in this scene; Iago is snide and underhand, Cassio gallant, Desdemona lively and loving, Othello confident, passionate and noble. We see the materials the villain has to work with. He is gaining ground steadily, poisoning the atmosphere and undermining the innocence and goodness of everyone around him. If there is any moment of pure happiness for Desdemona and Othello, it is located here. And yet this is the moment when Iago finds he can intervene, because he sees a way to use Cassio and Desdemona's interaction against them. The words are full of tension, and the physical juxtapositions of the characters add to this; Iago is downstage closest to the audience, a powerful physical presence who is dominant because he has the audience's ear. Are we forced to collude in Othello and Desdemona's downfall because Iago makes us tense? Do we begin to look for flaws as we listen to the romantic couple describing their love? We know we have reached a turning point because of the location: a war zone. The physical threat of the Turkish fleet may have been removed, but the villain, who poses a similar deadly threat to order and harmony is inside the camp. Finally, it is not simply Iago who makes us tense.

We know from her lines immediately prior to this extract that Desdemona is not as relaxed as she seems. Unlike Iago, Desdemona is open about her attempts to 'beguile / The thing I am by seeming otherwise' (II.1.122–3). Her innocent line reinforces our perception that nothing can ever be taken at face value in *Othello*.

TEXT 3 – V.2.222–79

This extract is taken from the final scene. Iago has been unmasked as a villain and Othello is forced to face the heinous nature of his crime.

CHECK THE FILM

Othello's fall from grace is conveyed in the final scenes of Parker's 1995 film when Othello appears in a black shirt and trousers. All the other male characters wear white shirts in the final scene.

> [IAGO *tries to stab* EMILIA.]
> GRATIANO: Fie! Your sword upon a woman?
> EMILIA: O thou dull Moor, that handkerchief thou speak'st of
> I found by fortune and did give my husband,
> For often, with a solemn earnestness   225
> – More than indeed belonged to such a trifle –
> He begged of me to steal't.
> IAGO: Villainous whore!
> EMILIA: She gave it Cassio? No, alas, I found it
> And I did give't my husband.
> IAGO: Filth, thou liest!
> EMILIA: By heaven I do not, I do not, gentlemen!   230
> O murderous coxcomb! what would such a fool
> Do with so good a wife?
>   [OTHELLO *runs at* IAGO. IAGO *stabs his wife.*]
> OTHELLO: Are there no stones in heaven
> But what serves for the thunder? Precious villain!
> GRATIANO: The woman falls, sure he hath killed his wife.
> EMILIA: Ay, ay; O lay me by my mistress' side.   *Exit* IAGO. 235
> GRATIANO: He's gone, but his wife's killed.
> MONTANO: 'Tis a notorious villain. Take you this weapon
> Which I have here recovered from the Moor;
> Come, guard the door without, let him not pass
> But kill him rather. I'll after that same villain,   240
> For 'tis a damned slave. *Exeunt* MONTANO *and* GRATIANO.
> OTHELLO: I am not valiant neither,
> But every puny whipster gets my sword.
> But why should honour outlive honesty?
> Let it go all.

CHECK THE BOOK

For a reading of Othello as noble hero, see A. C. Bradley's *Shakespearean Tragedy*.

EMILIA: What did thy song bode, lady?
Hark, canst thou hear me? I will play the swan   245
And die in music. [*Sings.*] Willow, willow, willow.
– Moor, she was chaste, she loved thee, cruel Moor,
So come my soul to bliss as I speak true!
So speaking as I think, alas, I die.   *She dies.*
OTHELLO: I have another weapon in this chamber,   250
It is a sword of Spain, the ice-brook's temper;
O, here it is. Uncle, I must come forth.
GRATIANO: [*within*]
If thou attempt it it will cost thee dear;
Thou hast no weapon, and perforce must suffer.
OTHELLO: Look in upon me then, and speak with me,   255
Or, naked as I am, I will assault thee.
     [*Enter* GRATIANO.]
GRATIANO: What is the matter?
OTHELLO: Behold, I have a weapon,
A better never did itself sustain
Upon a soldier's thigh. I have seen the day
That with this little arm and this good sword   260
I have made my way through more impediments
Than twenty times your stop: but, O vain boast,
Who can control his fate? 'Tis not so now.
Be not afraid, though you do see me weaponed:
Here is my journey's end, here is my butt   265
And very sea-mark of my utmost sail.
Do you go back dismayed? 'tis a lost fear:
Man but a rush against Othello's breast
And he retires. Where should Othello go?
Now: how dost thou look now? O ill-starred wench,   270
Pale as thy smock. When we shall meet at compt
This look of thine will hurl my soul from heaven
And fiends will snatch at it. Cold, cold, my girl,
Even like thy chastity. O cursed, cursed slave!
Whip me, ye devils,   275
From the possession of this heavenly sight!
Blow me about in winds, roast me in sulphur,
Wash me in steep-down gulfs of liquid fire!
O Desdemon! dead, Desdemon. Dead! O, O!

The confused physical violence that occurs at the beginning of this extract mirrors the mental confusion of the opening scene where Iago and Roderigo roused Brabantio from his bed. There is a sad irony in the fact that Othello, the great soldier is now reduced to a failed attempt on the '**notorious villain**' Iago's life; a sad end to his illustrious career. Emilia has revealed the truth about the handkerchief, the device that the whole plot has hung on and we now see the consequences of this truth. It is appropriate that 'honest' Iago is destroyed by his wife's real honesty. Our attention gradually comes to focus on Othello in this extract after Iago makes his temporary escape. Here the ensign is revealed as the despicable creature that the audience has known he is; he curses his wife roundly before wounding her and running off. This act of outrageous and unnatural cowardice seems to be the perfect physical expression of Iago's values; yet again he abuses a woman to try to preserve his own honour. His reductive oaths also seem to be the perfect verbal summation of the contempt he has shown towards the female characters throughout the play. But his defiance is typical too; even at this late moment he manages to escape. Even when he is captured Iago remains defiant and selfish: he will not speak.

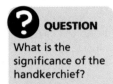

QUESTION

What is the significance of the handkerchief?

Emilia's role in this extract is to give voice to the audience's outrage at Desdemona's murder. She speaks plainly and passionately, defending Desdemona and guiding our responses to the heroine's death. The repetition in her lines is very affecting; she forces home the truth. Her echoing of Desdemona's willow song as she dies is designed to add to the pathos of the scene, as her previous anger was designed to move Othello towards recognition of his crime. Here Emilia proves for us the virtues of the plain speaker; which Othello recognises when he says, '**Are there no stones in heaven …**'. The wretched hero accepts Emilia's harsh words without demur because he recognises himself in her descriptions. We also see another Othello through Gratiano and Montano's responses to him. These two characters will provide the audience with a sense of closure at the end of this scene; here they begin to reassert the common-sense, masculine values of the Venetian state by insisting that the criminals pay for their wicked deeds. Their treatment of Othello suggests that the tragic hero has been reduced to the status of base villain. Montano and Gratiano treat him like a common criminal: '**let him not pass / But kill him rather**'. Gratiano suggests that Othello, like

Iago will be punished by the state, 'Thou hast no weapon, and perforce must suffer'. The disarming of Othello is symbolic. Here Othello is reduced to a nonentity; he is no longer a husband, and now the Venetians have taken his weapon he is no longer a soldier. In this extract Othello has been physically as well as mentally degraded, by others. This is fitting given his crime. But we also see that Shakespeare means to rehabilitate the tragic protagonist. Othello rises above Emilia and the Venetians' reductive versions of him because he readjusts his perception of himself.

Let us consider how Shakespeare begins to 'redeem' Othello. Firstly, Othello's vehement desire to be punished (rather than run away from the consequences of his actions as Iago does) goes in his favour. And Othello clearly feels that he deserves not just punishment, but torture: 'Whip me, ye devils' he begs, 'Blow me about in winds, roast me in sulphur / Wash me down in steep-gulfs of liquid fire!' Othello feels that he deserves to suffer the torments of hell for killing Desdemona. Some critics suggest that these lines prove that Othello knows that he is damned. His despair – 'Let it all go' – has also been interpreted as sinful. 'But why should honour outlive honesty?' is a key question which needs careful consideration. We may doubt Othello's conception of himself as honourable at this moment, but not for long. His question proves that he recognises his wife's honour, not his own and when we realise Othello has another weapon at line 250 we know that he will use this weapon on himself, and inflict the punishment he deserves. Desdemona's honesty will now lead her husband to an honourable suicide.

Shakespeare makes Othello impressive again in Act V Scene 2. T. S. Eliot has criticised Othello for trying to cheer himself up and dramatise himself in a self-aggrandising way in this final scene, but his 'Behold, I have a weapon' suggests overwhelming remorse and misery above all else. And Othello's use of the third person ('Where should Othello go?') does not so much suggest egotism as dislocation. Othello is lost: he has no wife or profession to sustain him. It is significant that he now prepares to use the weapon he has used to kill others on himself: he takes control of his own fate as he used to determine the fates of his enemies. The hero sees himself in a

QUESTION

Which other lines and images suggest 'dislocation' in this scene?

new and reduced light. He speaks of his 'little arm' and describes the 'impediments' he has made his way through on the battlefield not so much to boast, but to show that he knows he is diminished. Other lines suggest this too; he is as he says at his 'journey's end'. This phrase suggests Othello's weariness, as does his final use of a sea metaphor; 'here is my butt / And very sea-mark of my utmost sail' and the lines 'but a rush against Othello's breast / And he retires'. The hero is ready to die. Most importantly, although he despairs he makes a last brave attempt to exert himself. It is appropriate for Othello to refer back to his earlier life; Shakespeare wants to remind us how far this mighty, noble man has fallen. The fact that he is also now confined to his bedchamber by others (and by his own actions) also shows how he has been reduced. The once great warrior is now a prisoner. The location of this scene suggests claustrophobia and isolation. Although there are other characters on stage we also feel that Othello is really alone; he speaks to others briefly, but mostly speaks for himself, to prepare for his self-inflicted fate. If we accept that Othello is speaking of himself and not Iago when he calls out 'O cursed, cursed slave' (and there seems to be evidence to suggest he is, at the end of this sad speech Othello is thinking about himself and Desdemona, not Iago), we have further proof that Othello now feels himself unworthy. He also feels Desdemona's beauty and worthiness most agonisingly. Looking at her body he is overcome by woe: 'O Desdemon! dead, Desdemon. Dead! O, O!' These lines echo Othello's earlier despair; throughout the play the hero has been inarticulate in moments of extreme pain. When he refers to his wife as an 'ill-starred wench' and himself as a man unable to control his own fate we realise that the hero is moving closer to Desdemona and her values again. As in his final speech, Othello's last thoughts here are about the wife he has loved and lost.

CHECK THE BOOK

For comments on Act V Scene 2, in a section called 'The Final Act', see John Russell Brown's *Shakespeare: The Tragedies*.

This extract prepares us for Othello's last speech; it is the step he must take before killing himself. It is necessary that he explain his thoughts, feelings and remorse so that we will view him as a tragic hero rather than villain when he dies. We also need to hear him lament Desdemona's death and face himself. The differences between Othello and Iago must also be reasserted. During Acts IV and V Othello spiralled downwards, becoming more and more like

CHECK THE BOOK

For a negative reading of Othello's character, see F. R. Leavis' comments about the hero in *The Common Pursuit* 1962.

the ensign in his words and actions. When he begins to speak with some of his former nobility it is a poignant relief: we know that Iago's spell has been broken. Othello's measured calm is deeply affecting, especially given the hysteria and emotional tension of the earlier part of the scene. The 'cruel' Othello Emilia describes dies with the maid; now we know the hero's cruelty will be directed against himself because he has begun to square up to his shortcomings. This extract proves that the past is the past for Othello, but the present is so awful that there can be no future. Othello battles to make sense of what he has done. Although he confronts Iago briefly and is shortly to say that he feels he is not entirely to blame because he was 'Perplexed in the extreme' (V.2.344), we know that the hero accepts responsibility for his crime and will pay for it.

PART THREE

CRITICAL APPROACHES

CHARACTERISATION

OTHELLO

Othello is a play about opposites and opposition, and the many contradictions contained in the play are embodied in the tragic hero. We are aware from the opening scene that there are a number of possible views of Othello; all the characters hold very specific views of the tragic protagonist and we have to judge him in the light of the evidence they present, whilst also taking into account the hero's words, actions and idea of himself (which changes). The hero's two contradictory roles also need to be considered: we are required to respond to the Moor as both military man and lover-husband. There are other contradictions to accommodate. Othello occupies contradictory personal and political positions; he is a trusted foreign servant (an outsider), wielding power on behalf of the Venetian state, who then seeks to become an equal member of and participant in that society through marriage. He is also, of course, a black man in a white world.

Before he appears on stage we are led to believe that the Moor is professionally bombastic and proud and personally lascivious (Iago dwells on the general's abhorrent black sexuality in the opening scene). But Othello's appearance in Act I Scene 2 immediately contradicts this reductive assessment. Instead we see an impressive figure who displays a number of fine qualities; openness, sincerity, a natural authority, cool-headedness. Although Othello is not – unlike Shakespeare's other tragic protagonists – a monarch (King Lear), an aspiring monarch (Macbeth) or a displaced prince (Hamlet) he is nevertheless a worthy figure. Shakespeare stresses the paid mercenary's nobility. The Moor is the descendant of a royal line of kings (Othello refers to his birthright when he defends his right to marry Desdemona) and has been an impressive military commander. In the early scenes of the play we come to understand that Othello is self-confident but modest, just and generous. His attributes indicate that we should view him as a hero, as does his

CONTEXT

Africans of both sexes were a visible minority in seventeenth-century London, and there were interracial couples. It has even been suggested that Shakespeare knew a black prostitute who lived in the Cripplegate area of the city.

customary mode of speech (Othello almost always speaks in verse and is a fine rhetorician, despite his protestations to the contrary).

The focus in this play is, as many critics have suggested, domestic: Othello's previous history, the Turkish invasion and machinations of the Venetian state provide the backdrop to an essentially private tragedy. Although the play focuses on the terrible consequences of sexual jealousy, we must not ignore the wider worldly or political dimension of Othello's tragedy. Othello is proud of his profession and as many critics have noted, his reputation as a soldier is an essential part of the hero's conception of himself. Indeed, some would argue that the impulse for revenge comes directly out of his need to recover his reputation. A Jacobean audience would have understood the weight Othello attaches to his reputation: a man's honour was extremely important and his wife's chastity was an integral part of it. When he fears that he has been cuckolded the hero doubts himself and is forced to accommodate a new role, that of duped husband, which his pride will not allow him to accept. It is also possible to argue that Othello's marriage is a political act (a black soldier marrying a white aristocrat cannot be viewed in any other way, even if, as many would argue, the play suggests it is a good match) and that the precarious situation in Cyprus contributes directly to Othello's downfall (Iago is able to take advantage of the fact that Cyprus is in a state of uneasiness following the threat of invasion). When considering Othello's blackness it is important to remember that the racist descriptions of the hero are all offered by characters whose judgement we do not trust and that Desdemona is not coerced into marriage; she defends her choice with her dying breath.

Let us consider Othello's roles and how they are perceived by others more closely. 'Valiant Othello' (I.3.49) commands the respect of other respected figures (the Duke of Venice, Montano). Even Brabantio admired the Moor as a soldier before he became his son-in-law. Although we do not see much evidence of his leadership in Cyprus (except in the aftermath of the 'quarrel' between Roderigo and Cassio) we do not doubt that Othello is a conscientious soldier; he attempts to ensure that the carousing at his wedding festivities does not get out of hand and inspects the fortifications in the town carefully in Act III Scene 2. We are also encouraged to view

Othello's heroic past – as Desdemona and Brabantio do – as
intriguing. Othello possesses a mythical, monumental quality that
cannot be denied. He speaks and acts powerfully and in a way that
inspires confidence in his character throughout the first two acts of
the play.

The difficulty comes – and not just for Brabantio – in accepting
Othello wholeheartedly as a perfect wooer, lover and husband. Part
of this difficulty comes from the fact that he has married
Desdemona in secret; a covert act that sits uncomfortably with
Othello's protestation that he has nothing to hide after the marriage.
However, we are not encouraged to dwell on the elopement itself
because it quickly becomes clear that Desdemona was 'half the
wooer' (I.3.176) and the couple speak clearly and honestly about
their love, to the council and to each other. Their meeting in Cyprus
reveals the intensity and sincerity of their mutual affection. We do
not doubt that Othello and Desdemona make a worthy couple. The
Duke of Venice seems to recognise Othello's suitability as a wooer
when he says, 'I think this tale would win my daughter too'
(I.3.172); he then seeks to reassure Brabantio, 'Your son-in-law is
far more fair than black' (I.3.291). However, there are tensions and
contradictions that must be admitted, and these tensions arise out of
Othello's attempts to reconcile his roles as soldier and husband. In
the senate scene Desdemona insists that she married Othello to live
with him and enjoy her marital 'rites' (I.3.258), while her husband
declares that marriage will not distract him from his duties and that
he is not prey to sexual passion. We gradually come to question the
hero's self-knowledge on this point; he may be a resolute and
capable general, but the events of the play suggest that he is out of
his depth in matters of the heart. We also realise that Othello's
sexuality is very important, regardless of the hero's insistence that
he is a sedate middle-aged man who is past the excesses of youthful
passion; not only because Desdemona insists on her husband's
sexual attractiveness, but also because Othello himself eagerly
anticipates the consummation of their marriage (see II.3.8–11).
However, the mutual erotic attraction between husband and wife
dissuades us from accepting Iago's stereotyped portrait of the Moor
as a lascivious 'black ram' (I.1.87). Othello's sexuality is not sinister;
he has not had to force his attentions on Desdemona.

> **CONTEXT**
>
> Ben Jonson's
> comedy *Every Man
> in His Humour*,
> in which
> Shakespeare is
> believed to have
> acted, includes a
> jealous husband
> called Thorello.
> Perhaps this is
> where
> Shakespeare got
> the name for his
> Moorish hero.

When Othello greets Desdemona in Cyprus we get the first hint that the hero is overwhelmed by his love for wife; he declares that he is almost too happy. Then in Act III Scene 3 he says that he fears chaos when he is away from Desdemona. We are now forced to recognise that Othello cannot master his powerful romantic and erotic feelings; he is in the grip of emotions that he cannot control, even before Iago sets to work on him. Put simply, we might be tempted to feel that the rational soldier has become a blind lover. Many critics would suggest that his inability to come to terms with his new role as husband contributes to Othello's tragedy. We might also say that the qualities that served him so well as a soldier contribute to Othello's demise; his decisiveness leads him to seek 'ocular proof' (III.3.363) and then when he is presented with that proof his decision to pursue a bloody course is made swiftly.

But it is not quite this simple. Othello suffers acutely from Act III Scene 3 onwards and does not perhaps give into his feelings of jealousy as swiftly as some critics suggest; he tries many times to persuade himself that Desdemona is honest and has second thoughts about murdering her as late as the final scene. And we cannot ignore Iago's powerful presence. Othello may have a propensity towards jealousy (critics are divided on this issue) but the ensign is immensely plausible and cunning and Othello has no reason not to trust him. There is a good deal of evidence in the play to indicate that the hero is pushed towards tragedy by a ruthless 'demi-devil' (V.2.298), who takes advantage of his noble nature. We know just how powerful Iago's influence is because Othello begins to speak and think like the ensign in the second half of the play when his imagination is polluted. We are forced to come to terms with the idea that the hero is not wholly noble; he is also capable of savagery and crudeness.

Undoubtedly the transformation in Othello is troublesome and awkward questions remain. Why does Othello trust Iago more than he trusts his beloved wife? Why does he believe the worst of Cassio, who has been a trusted friend and colleague? But we understand that Othello's conception of himself has been challenged; do not forget that Iago cruelly reminds him that he is an outsider and also addresses him as an ordinary, foolish cuckold (see IV.1.65–73).

CONTEXT

At the time that *Othello* was first performed, the African slave trade was already established. In the 1550s Elizabethan adventurers had set out to the coast of Africa, where they raided the villages and kidnapped some of the inhabitants, bringing them back to England. Othello himself describes how he was briefly imprisoned as a slave.

Given his pride, the hero finds this intolerable. Some critics have suggested that Othello's readiness to believe Iago is a sign that the hero is naive and rather stupid, and that lack of intellect contributes to his tragedy. Others suggest that he is not only out of his depth in love but is also, because of his background, utterly unable to comprehend the subtle and sophisticated society that he has married into; these critics suggest that the Moor is essentially a noble savage. But these readings are unsatisfactory (and racist) and they also fly in the face of textual evidence. By the time that he descends into murderous jealousy we are well acquainted with the noble Othello and also recognise that he has been 'ensnar'd' (V.2.299). Othello may begin to act out part of the stereotypical black role assigned to him by Iago in the second half of the play when he speaks and acts cruelly, but we are constantly aware that he is directly under his ensign's poisonous influence and is being pulled in many directions. Surely his preoccupation with honour and chastity are the obsessions not of a savage, but of a virtuous character who understands and subscribes to the codes of his adopted society? We might also feel that his desire to revenge himself on Cassio and Desdemona is the terrible result of Othello's attempt to combine his roles as soldier and lover. When he fears that he has been betrayed by his wife he says woefully, 'Othello's occupation's gone!' (III.3.360); it is almost as if Desdemona was the prize he earned for his military victories. She has perhaps replaced his career as the source of his pride and honour; no wonder he feels her loss so keenly. It is also possible to argue that it is his insistence on the importance of his honour that both redeems and damns Othello.

In the final scene he constantly has an eye on his own reputation, which seems inappropriate to many critics. However, others would argue that because he believes he is preventing Desdemona from deceiving other men Othello is not entirely incorrect to refer to himself an 'honourable murderer' (V.2.291). Othello also reminds us of his former services to the state in his final speech; Shakespeare perhaps wishes us to remember that the hero was a worthy man before he was ensnared by Iago. When he commits suicide the tragic protagonist also reaffirms his honour. Othello courageously takes his own life to pay for the crime of killing his honest wife; in his final lines and final act he is perhaps finally able to reconcile his two

> **CONTEXT**
>
> Critics have suggested that Othello became 'tawny' rather than black in stage productions in the 1800s. This was to prevent the role from being linked to the idea of slavery.

contradictory roles; the soldier kills the faulty lover. So, while it is
impossible to condone his actions in Act V Scene 3 it is possible to
sympathise with and pity the fallen hero. (For further comments on
Othello's race see **Images and themes**.)

DESDEMONA

Desdemona occupies contradictory positions in *Othello*; she is both
'half the wooer' (I.3.176) (an active female who makes her own
choices – to marry Othello and to defend Cassio) and the passive
prey or victim. She is abused by four male characters in the play: her
father Brabantio, who misjudges and then rejects her; Roderigo,
who seeks an adulterous liaison with her; Iago, who uses her cruelly
to further his own revenge; and her husband Othello, who ignores
her protestations of innocence and then silences her. We might say
that *Othello* shows us how a woman's character and reputation can
be manipulated and distorted by men. Like Othello, Desdemona
contradicts early descriptions of her character when she first
appears in the play. Her father tells us that she is his 'jewel' (I.3.196),
'a maiden never bold, / of spirit' (I.3.95–6), modest and opposed to
marriage, afraid to look on Othello. She emerges from his
descriptions as an innocent, shrinking, girlish figure, so we are
unprepared for the forthright, brave young woman we see in the
senate scene. Desdemona is not afraid to assert her rights as a
married woman and insists openly that she is ready for a sexual
relationship. There are other exchanges in the play that suggest
Desdemona's sexuality. Some critics wonder at her participation in
the crude talk with Iago in Act II Scene 1, and her reference to
Lodovico in Act IV Scene 3 can seem troublesome. But the
heroine's active sexuality is necessary to the play; Iago is able to
make a great deal out of the fact that she deceived her father in order
to choose her own husband.

But it is important to remember that although Desdemona has
disobeyed her father, she expects to submit to her husband's
authority. She states this explicitly when she says, 'My heart's
subdued / Even to the utmost pleasure of my lord:' (I.3.251–2).
Those who accuse Desdemona of being an assertive nag also ignore
the fact that she only assumes the role of domestic harpy in order to
bring about a reconciliation between her husband and Cassio, which

QUESTION

How far is
Desdemona
responsible for her
own death?

she believes is in Othello's best professional interests. Her 'nagging'
is playful and loving, her anxiousness about Othello's health
touching. But Desdemona is not the faultless paragon Cassio
describes so gallantly; she lies to Othello about the handkerchief
(understandably; he frightens her with his serious talk about its
magical properties). However, by this point, we know that Iago's
sinister plots are working, and the heroine becomes increasingly
vulnerable and impotent in each scene that follows. When her
husband strikes her publicly she reproaches him briefly ('I have not
deserved this', IV.1.240) but then accepts – and defends – his
authority over her, as we see from her discussion with Emilia at the
start of Act IV Scene 3. She asserts her loving loyalty and questions
Othello bravely in Act IV Scene 2 (see IV.2.30–89) but is reduced to
dumb misery when her husband calls her 'that cunning whore of
Venice' (IV.2.91): 'nor answer have I none' she says woefully
(IV.2.105), remarking – girlishly – that she is 'a child at chiding'
(IV.2.116). Desdemona's unworldly innocence is emphasised again
in Act IV Scene 3: she cannot believe that a woman would choose to
commit adultery. Ultimately the virtuous Desdemona refuses to
blame Othello for her unhappiness: she declares it is her 'wretched
fortune' (IV.2.129). She has learned that 'men are not gods'
(III.4.149) and this is a disappointment to her. But while
Desdemona submits willingly to the man she chose, she dies
valiantly, fighting to be allowed to live and asserting her right to
defend herself. She has to be literally silenced. Her final words are
intriguing and contradictory. There are many ways of reading them.
Has Desdemona taken control of her own fate? Is she trying to
protect her husband in death as she sought to defend him in life? Or
are these the selfless words of a powerless figure, who acts out the
role of innocent victim? However we interpret her final words, we
will certainly feel that the heroine's apparent self-abnegation in Act
V Scene 2 contradicts her earlier assertiveness; Desdemona has
indeed become a sacrifice.

IAGO

Iago is a compelling and sophisticated villain. He is part **vice**, part
Machiavel and like Shakespeare's Richard III, seems to be
inherently evil. Iago revels in his ability to dissemble and destroy.
But while Iago to some extent enjoys having an audience (Roderigo)

QUESTION

Is Iago, as
Coleridge
suggested, an
example of
'motiveless
malignity'?

and outlines his plots clearly, he is also rather mysterious and unfathomable, especially when he refuses to speak at the end of *Othello*. Some critics have suggested that Iago is a cold-blooded creature. He has also been accused of possessing a detached 'motiveless malignity' (see Coleridge's comments in **Critical history**); in fact, we are offered a number of reasons for the ensign's plots and plans. At times Iago does perhaps seem to be hunting down his motives, but this does not detract from their existence. We are presented with a villain who is adept at quick-witted improvisation (like so many Shakespearean villains). Like Edmund in *King Lear*, Iago fashions his plots out of the material he has at hand.

CONTEXT

Orson Welles, director and lead actor in his own 1952 film version of the play, felt that Iago must be motivated by impotence.

So what motivates Iago? Professional jealousy is his initial motive for disgracing Cassio; but he also admits that he is personally envious of the '**daily beauty**' in the lieutenant's life (V.1.19). In addition to this, he says that he believes Cassio has committed adultery with his wife, Emilia. Iago's relationship with Roderigo is driven by callous acquisitiveness and when his '**purse**' (I.3.381) becomes a dangerous inconvenience, he kills him. His motives for destroying Othello's happiness are also driven by negative impulses. Iago is eaten up with sexual jealousy. He says he hates Othello because he suspects the general has "twixt my sheets … done my office' (I.1.386–7). After this soliloquy in Act I Scene 1 it comes as no surprise to hear him say '**nothing can, nor shall content my soul, / Till I am evened with him, wife for wife**' (II.1.296–7). And because of this gnawing paranoia, Iago determines to use Desdemona's goodness to '**enmesh 'em all**' (II.3.357). He also holds a grudge against Othello for promoting Cassio over him. We might add misogyny and racism to the motives outlined here; although he never says explicitly that he hates women or foreigners, his unceedingly low opinion of them, which comes across in many of his speeches, suggests that Iago wants to degrade those he despises. Many critics have noted that Iago is propelled to revenge by feelings of frustration and loathing; he wants those (Cassio and Othello) who have, as he sees it, wounded him personally and professionally, to suffer in the way that he suffers. Like Othello, he is immensely proud, but his pride is laced with sly vindictiveness while the Moor is generous and open. He is also self-contained, egotistical and independent. These qualities help him in his treacherous quest.

Iago is successful because he can play a number of roles convincingly, and is able to adapt his tone and style to suit any occasion. He enjoys his ability to hoodwink others into believing he is honest. With Cassio he is bluff, coarse and genial. He also offers the lieutenant plausible practical advice; he adopts a similar sympathetic approach when he deals with Desdemona in Act IV Scene 2. With Montano and Lodovico he makes a point of stressing that he has Othello's and the Venetian state's best interests at heart. There seems to be an absence of ego in all his dealings with these characters, who are socially and professionally superior to him. But this is deliberate: with his inferiors (Roderigo and Emilia) Iago can afford to be less circumspect and selfless. His exchanges with Roderigo reveal that the villain as a self-serving and materialistic cynic; although we know that Iago needs to persuade the foolish Venetian that he has good reason to be dissatisfied, there is not that much difference between the Iago who speaks alone in his soliloquies and the Iago who gulls Roderigo. Both are dismissive, mean-spirited and boastful. His brusque exchange with Emilia in Act III Scene 3 and his threats in Act V Scene 2 are also similar; Iago only bothers to speak to his wife pleasantly when he thinks she has something he wants, otherwise his tone is cold and contemptuous.

His dealings with Othello reveal Iago's real skill. His relationship with the general is complex and fascinating. Some critics suggest he seeks to replace Desdemona in the Moor's affections because he has latent homosexual feelings; although this is debatable, Iago certainly sets out to prove to Othello that his 'love' is more honourable than the 'super-subtle' Venetian's (I.3.357). Gradually, the ensign assumes the control and power we associate with Othello; so successfully that the Moor even begins to speak and think like his petty, reductive inferior. How does the 'inhuman dog' (V.1.62) destroy the mind, soul and body of the noble, valiant Moor? The ensign makes his general believe that he is loyal, conscientious and noble minded (these are of course – ironically – Othello's best qualities). He pretends that he would like to cudgel Othello's detractors in Act I Scene 2, seems most anxious about the consequences of the brawl in Act II Scene 3 and then hesitatingly describes his 'friend' Cassio's part in the evening's events. His show of reluctance in Act III Scene 3 is also devastatingly effective. By pretending that he doesn't wish

> **CONTEXT**
>
> A Freudian interpretation of the play might suggest that Iago is subconsciously in love with Othello. This is how Laurence Olivier played the part of Iago. At the line 'I am your own forever' (III.3.486), he kissed his Othello (Ralph Richardson) on the lips.

Iago's
Machiavellian
antecedents in
Shakespeare's
plays include the
corrupt and
corrupting *Richard
III*, who, like Iago,
takes the audience
in through his use
of asides.

to divulge his thoughts he manoeuvres himself into a position where he is able to poison Othello's mind thoroughly. Iago has an acute eye for his victims' weaknesses or flaws and exploits them mercilessly: he is puppetmaster. Iago's role-playing enables him to become stage manager and dramatist, controlling his victims' fates increasingly effortlessly, until he is unmasked by his wife, whose obedience he (ironically) took for granted. A good example of his setting up, directing and then decoding events for his victims occurs in Act IV Scene 1, when Iago persuades Othello to eavesdrop on his conversation with Cassio. The Moor is not only told what to do; he is also told how to interpret Cassio's looks and gestures. Note Iago's confident use of commands:

> *encave yourself*
> And *mark* the fleers, the gibes, and notable scorns
> That dwell in every region of his face;
> For *I will make him* tell the tale anew
> Where, how, how oft, how long, and when,
> He hath and is again to cope your wife.
>
> (IV.1.82–7, my emphasis)

**CHECK
THE FILM**

In the 1990 and
1995 TV/film
productions, Iago
speaks directly to
camera in close-up,
drawing the viewer
in. Many soliloquies
are whispered
coolly and
ferociously, through
clenched teeth. The
line 'I hate the
Moor' (I.3.384) is
emphasised slowly
and very bitterly by
both Iagos,
McKellen and
Branagh.

These lines reveal another of Iago's characteristics, his cruel vulgarity. He is gleeful and determined as he tortures Othello with the details of Cassio's supposed liaison with his wife; he explores Desdemona's supposed infidelity as carefully and thoroughly as he describes his motives; every fictional look, word, gesture and meeting is relayed in detail by Iago during Acts III and IV. He is a supremely effective storyteller, as we see in his description of the night he pretends to have spent sharing a bed with Cassio in Act III Scene 3. Gradually, Othello becomes Iago's unwitting audience as well as his puppet. Even Cassio seems to become infected by Iago's cynical and misogynistic outlook; in Act IV Scene 1 he speaks of Bianca cuttingly and coarsely, acting out the role that Iago has cast him in. Roderigo employs a theatrical metaphor when he grumbles about his lack of progress with Desdemona. He accuses Iago of deceiving him with these words: 'your words and performance are no kin together' (IV.2.184–5). The wonderful and alarming irony of this is that the foolish Roderigo speaks the truth without having any idea that he has done so. As usual Iago talks Roderigo round in a very short time, leading him away with these decisive words: 'I will show you such necessity in his [Cassio's] death, that you shall think yourself bound to put it on him' (IV.2.241–43). He is also loquacious with Roderigo. But the ensign also makes effective use of brevity, prevarication and insinuation, as we see in his early dealings with Othello. In spite of his gifts and acute assessment of others, many critics would argue that the villain has a very limited understanding of those around him. Others have suggested that Iago recognises others' virtues but perceives them as foolish weaknesses.

Although it is possible to analyse Iago's methods and motives, the villain remains somewhat inscrutable. We feel as if we get close to him because he draws us in through his use of asides and **soliloquies**, but at the end of the play he somehow eludes us when he refuses to speak. We are tempted to question the validity of Iago's motives and are perhaps drawn to considering what really makes him tick; what lies beneath that corrupt and cynical surface? We might also question the villain's self-knowledge and judgement. Some critics feel that Iago's reductive world view indicates that he is a petty character whose cleverness is limited; the end of the play proves that you cannot hoodwink everyone all of the time: Iago is foolish to believe that he can. But others who are more sure of Iago's destructive power point to his silence as proof that the 'demi-devil' (V.2.298) has not been vanquished. When he takes refuge in silence Iago asserts his power in another horrible way; Othello wishes to know why he has been 'Perplexed in the extreme' (V.2.344) and yet the 'hellish villain' (V.2.366) refuses to tell him. · Our final assessment of Iago must acknowledge his terrible achievements as well as his ultimate failure; he succeeds in destroying a marriage and two noble characters, as well as his wife and Roderigo.

 CHECK THE BOOK

For a detailed discussion of Iago as alienated, triumphant villain, and an exploration of the villain's motives, see W. H. Auden's essay 'The Joker in the Pack' in John Wain (ed.), *Othello: Casebook*.

CASSIO

Like many of the other characters in *Othello*, Cassio – another of Iago's victims – can be viewed from different perspectives. In Act I Scene 1 we are offered a belittling portrait of him by the envious ensign; he is an inexperienced soldier, a mere 'arithmetician' (I.1.18) who has been promoted beyond his deserving. We are also informed

that Cassio is a Florentine – which makes him an outsider like
Othello – and 'A fellow almost damned in a fair wife' (I.1.20). This
seems to be a throwaway remark in the first scene; but Cassio's
appeal to women is important. Iago is able to manipulate Cassio's
image in the same way that he manipulates Desdemona's; he takes
advantage of the lieutenant's courtesy, recognising that this victim's
weakness lies in the fact that he is 'handsome, young and hath all
those requisites in him that folly and green minds look after'; in
short, Iago is able to make Cassio look as if he is 'framed to make
women false' (I.3.397). It is possible to feel that his gallantry is a
little overworked on occasions, but essentially the lieutenant is open
and sincere in his praise of Desdemona.

**CHECK
THE FILM**

In Parker's 1995 film
version of *Othello*,
Nathaniel Parker,
who plays Cassio, is
handsome and
genial, but he
forgets Bianca's
name. What point
do you think the
director was trying
to make?

In stark contrast to the role of lady-killer that Iago casts him in,
Cassio comes across as something of an innocent to begin with. In
the first scenes in which he appears he is 'Good Michael', 'a proper
man', (II.3.1 and I.3.391) an attractive character, especially when
compared with the cynical ensign. He denies any knowledge of
Othello's elopement in Act I Scene 2 and clearly does not share
Iago's crude interpretation of events. In Act II Scene 3 Iago attempts
to discuss the consummation of Othello's marriage with Cassio in
rather vulgar terms (see II.3.13–25) but the lieutenant refuses to be
drawn into this saucy delineation of Desdemona's charms, insisting
simply and courteously that she is 'a most exquisite lady' (II.3.18).
His frank admission that he has a weak head for drink immediately
after this conversation also suggests his open honesty and
innocence, as does his swift and eloquent remorse once he has lost
his position. Like Othello, he is wretched at the thought that his
reputation has been sullied.

Later in the play Cassio's proper appearance seems to conceal some
unsavoury qualities, which are revealed through his interaction with
Bianca. His treatment of his mistress is rather callous and it is hard
not to judge him harshly when he tells her to be gone because he
does not want to be found 'womaned' (III.4.194). Perhaps Cassio
might even be accused of using women in the same way that Iago
does; he initially hopes to persuade Emilia to plead with
Desdemona to intervene on his behalf and then allows Desdemona
to take up his cause. We might also feel that his reluctance to face

Othello reveals a rather weak character. He may not 'steal away so guilty-like' (III.3.38) as Iago suggests, but is it not rather spineless to leave the assertion of his worth entirely to Desdemona?

However, it is essential that Cassio hang back for the purposes of the plot and we cannot blame the lieutenant entirely for the course of action he follows: Iago has persuaded him that his best hopes lie in winning Desdemona over first. And a casual liaison with a young courtesan is not enough to detract from his good qualities. We have to remember the 'daily beauty' (V.1.19) of his life that Iago detests so much. It is after all Cassio who – ironically – replaces Othello as governor of Cyprus at the end of the play. We are forced to conclude that his worthiness outweighs his weakness.

EMILIA

Emilia shares some of her mistress's qualities; she is a loyal wife who seeks to please her husband (she gives Iago Desdemona's handkerchief because she knows he covets it) and feels that it proper that she obeys and submits to her spouse. But like Desdemona Emilia also defends herself and her sex. She replies sharply when Iago derides women in Act II Scene 1: 'You shall not write my praise' (II.1.116). In Act III Scene 4 we see that Emilia is more realistic about male–female relationships than Desdemona. Discussing marriage and men she says:

> 'Tis not a year or two shows us a man.
> They are all but stomachs, and we all but food:
> They eat us hungrily, and when they are full
> They belch us.   (III.4.104–7)

It is impossible to imagine Desdemona speaking in this down-to-earth, practical and vulgar tone.

As Desdemona becomes less assertive in the second half of the play Emilia's role becomes more important. She becomes her mistress's energetic defender, voicing the audience's outrage at the treatment Desdemona receives. She is sharp-witted, describing Othello's destructive jealousy accurately. She is also wise without knowing it when she says angrily 'The Moor's abused by some most villainous

CHECK THE BOOK
For a feminist reading of the play see Marilyn French's essay in John Drakakis (ed.), *Shakespearean Tragedy*.

CHECK THE NET

For reviews of character, context etc. go to **www. absolute shakespeare.com/ guides**.

knave' (IV.2.141). In the final scene Emilia becomes the voice of truth and finally stops Iago's evil progress. It is impossible not to agree with some of her harsh judgements of Othello and we know that she is absolutely right to betray Iago. Her final lines reconfirm her own and her mistress's honesty:

> So come my soul to bliss as I speak true!
> So speaking as I think, alas, I die.   (V.2.248–9)

Yet there are aspects of Emilia's characterisation that give us pause. Why does she give the handkerchief to Iago when she does not know why he wants it and when she also knows that her mistress will 'run mad' when she discovers it has gone (III.3.321)? Does she also perhaps suspect her husband before she finally speaks out? Consider these lines from Act V Scene 2:

> Villainy, villainy, villainy!
> I think upon't: I think I smell't: O villainy!
> I thought so then: I'll kill myself for grief!   (V.2.187–9)

Some critics argue that Emilia has suppressed her suspicions, that her desire to 'speak true' comes too late (V.2.248). Others point to her horrified repeated question 'My husband?' (V.2.138, 141, 146) as proof that she is guiltless. Her pragmatism about men and women is also perhaps not far enough removed from Iago's cynicism. We must be cautious about her defence of adultery in Act III Scene 4. She speaks theoretically here, but her casual acceptance of sin is perhaps an indication that Emilia is too crude a moraliser to be relied on completely as a judge of Othello's character in the final scene.

BRABANTIO

In spite of the fact that he has clearly been abused, some modern audiences find it difficult to view Brabantio favourably. A Jacobean audience may have felt his wrongs more deeply, recognising Desdemona's elopement as an assault on patriarchy; like Juliet, the treasured daughter denies her father's right to dispose of her in marriage as he sees fit. Brabantio sees this as a 'gross revolt' (I.1.132) and it leads to his death (we are informed that his daughter's marriage was 'mortal' to him, V.2.203). So why is it perhaps difficult to sympathise with the abused father? Brabantio has not been an unsympathetic parent; he has allowed his daughter to reject suitable matches and holds her in high esteem (his descriptions of Desdemona in the senate scene may not fit with the confident young woman we see when she appears, but Brabantio recognises her virtues). We also understand that there has been domestic harmony in Brabantio's wealthy home until the elopement occurs: Othello has been entertained often and Brabantio has been a friendly host.

The senator is an important man used to commanding; ironically, these are qualities he shares with his son-in-law Othello. We are led to believe that he is a valuable member of the council: the Duke says that he was missed during the discussions about the Turkish invasion. We might feel, however, that Brabantio is too harsh, even though his pessimism about his daughter's marriage proves correct; he rejects Desdemona rather brutally when he finds he has been disobeyed and will not accept a black son-in-law. He is materialistic; his use of the word 'jewel' (I.3.196) to describe Desdemona suggests that he regards his daughter as a possession. Brabantio insults Othello when he accuses him of witchcraft, and his warning to the Moor, 'She has deceived her father, and may thee' (I.3.294) strikes a sour note. We might feel that his judgement is questionable; he has failed to recognise his daughter's true character and also refuses to acknowledge Othello's worth (unlike the rest of the Venetian senators). His immovable unkindness to the lovers prevents us from feeling for him wholeheartedly. His impatient and dismissive tone with Roderigo in Act I Scene 1 might also count against him; particularly when viewed in relation to his later comment about this failed suitor. It is impossible to believe that Roderigo deserves Desdemona. Ultimately we might see Brabantio as another of Iago's victims; his unfavourable view of his son-in-law is perhaps constructed by the ensign. Like all the other characters in the play Brabantio finds it difficult to distinguish between appearances and reality and suffers as a result.

CHECK THE FILM

In Parker's 1995 film Brabantio's bitter lines 'She has deceived her father …' are repeated in flashback late in the play, showing their importance and significance for Othello.

RODERIGO

Roderigo is a gull and a simpleton, whose primary role is to enable the audience to gain insight into Iago's modus operandi. In his exchanges with the 'poor trash of Venice' (II.1.301) the ensign's cynical world view is revealed. As a disappointed suitor Roderigo also represents the 'curled darlings' (I.2.68) that Desdemona has rejected, providing us with a point of comparison with Othello, the successful wooer. However, even if we partially sympathise with the view that Othello proves to be, as Emilia suggests a 'most filthy bargain' (V.2.153), we can hardly agree with Brabantio when he says that he wishes he had given his daughter to Roderigo rather than see her married to the exotic outsider. Roderigo is not worthy of Desdemona. He exercises extremely poor judgement and his actions are generally despicable; he shares responsibility with Iago for prejudicing Brabantio's view of his daughter's elopement, eggs Cassio on to a fight which disrupts order in Cyprus and then participates in an attempt on the lieutenant's life without feeling entirely convinced that his intended victim deserves to die. We also question Roderigo's continued pursuit of Desdemona; he blindly chases an adulterous liaison and thinks that he can buy his inamorata's favours with jewels. Roderigo's racist descriptions of Othello also go against him.

? QUESTION

What do *you* think – is Roderigo a victim or a villain?

However, there are grounds for believing that Roderigo is corrupted and not wholly bad, merely weak; lacking resolution or volition, he even has to be directed off stage on a number of occasions. He is suspicious of Iago, but allows himself to be talked round. He is the ensign's first victim. It is possible to see Roderigo as another outsider in *Othello*; Iago keeps him on the fringes of the action in Venice and Cyprus, ensuring that he remains powerless. Roderigo can also be played as a comic figure: his description of being cudgelled can be amusing. Roderigo's miserable end seems a cruel fate; like Othello he realises the truth about his manipulator too late and pays the price.

BIANCA

Like Desdemona, Bianca is used and abused by the male characters in *Othello*. She is only seen in relation to men and is always in a vulnerable position; Iago maligns her mercilessly in Act V Scene 2 to distract attention from himself and Cassio is prepared to dally with but not marry her. Critics question whether Bianca is in fact a prostitute but Cassio's description of himself as her 'customer' (IV.1.120) suggests that she may well be a courtesan. She is not, however, an ignoble or 'low' character and we feel some sympathy for her. Bianca can be compared with both Desdemona and Emilia and shares some of their qualities. Her relationship with Cassio is less idealistic than the Othello-Desdemona match, but she is an affectionate and genuine partner. She too is accused falsely of treacherous behaviour (by Iago). Her unfounded jealousy mirrors Othello's; but because she has no power she cannot assert her rights as the wronged party. The handkerchief causes Bianca the same anxiety that it causes the hero. It is worth considering the view of women expressed by Iago in relation to all the female characters in *Othello*: do any of them provide proof that they are weak minded, foolish, petty or inconstant? There is a strong sense that the women in this play are hapless victims; Bianca, the least powerful figure in the play, is – ironically – the only female survivor.

LANGUAGE AND STRUCTURE

LANGUAGE IN *OTHELLO*

Elizabethan and Jacobean dramatists used language to establish and build dramatic atmosphere, to define time, place and character. But in *Othello*, language is not simply the medium by which the drama is conveyed: in this play language *is* action. Othello 'falls' because he believes a man whose every utterance is deceptive. When the hero is taken in by false words, tragedy is the result. This play shows us the power of words; we watch as characters construct their own and others' identities through language, and exert power either by speaking, remaining silent or silencing others.

Othello is written in **blank verse** and prose. Blank verse consists of unrhymed iambic pentameters, with five stressed syllables and five unstressed syllables to each line. Shakespeare uses this traditional form flexibly, however, varying the pace of his writing to achieve specific effects. He also creates specific idioms for each of his characters. If we look at the language of Othello and Iago we can see how the dramatist creates not only character, but also the theme of opposition which is central to the play. From his opening speeches in Act I, Scenes 2 and 3 it is clear that Othello's characteristic idiom is dignified, measured blank verse. This is appropriate, given his status in the play. His use of blank verse also helps establish his heroism.

 CHECK THE NET
For questions (supplied by students and interested general readers) and answers on Shakespeare's works try visiting this site: **www.talkingto. co.uk/ttws**. It includes a number of questions and answers on Othello. It is a good, accessible and interesting site that covers a range of issues relevant to A-level students.

CONTEXT

G. Wilson-Knight has described Othello's speech as 'highly coloured … stately … rich in sound and phrase'. He also suggests that Othello's speech displays a 'uniquely soldierly precision' and 'a peculiar chastity and serenity of thought'. His famous lines convey these qualities: 'Keep up your bright swords, for the dew will rust them' (I.2.59).

Othello speaks clearly and purposefully. His authority also comes across in these lines, and there is a sense of both danger and beauty – entirely appropriate to the speaker – in his references to 'bright swords' and 'dew'. We are immediately aware that the hero is an impressive character and a powerful speaker. This power is reinforced in the next scene when Othello uses words not just to defend his elopement with Desdemona, but also to enable him to keep her; if he does not speak convincingly the 'bloody book of law' (I.3.68) may deprive him of his wife. Desdemona acknowledges her husband's rhetorical power when she enters. We already know that she was seduced by his storytelling; now we discover that she uses the same dignified and purposeful idiom that he employs. Through their shared speech patterns Shakespeare conveys the harmony and mutual affection of Othello and Desdemona's match; the lovers are as Iago expresses it 'well tun'd' (II.1.198) at this point. Each of Othello's long speeches in this scene could be compared to a poem; expressing the nobility and romance we come to associate with the tragic protagonist. Many critics see Othello as Shakespeare's most 'poetic' hero, a fitting judgement given the fact that we focus of the protagonist's experiences of love in this play. But Othello does not just speak of his love poetically; he also speaks of his glorious career as a soldier in the same vein, thus establishing himself as a great military man. The orderliness of his verse suggests not just his confidence, but also the fact that we, and the senate are wise to trust in his composure and reason. Linked to this, Othello's reference to and pride in his 'estimation' (I.3.275), also help to convey a sense of the hero's worth; while also suggesting that the way in which you are perceived by others – your reputation – is going to be an important theme in this play.

When Othello begins to see himself and his wife through Iago's eyes and is corrupted by Iago's idiom, his stately style begins to break down. At his lowest point, just before he falls to the ground in an epileptic fit, Othello's words convey his agitation:

> Lie with her, lie on her? We say lie on her,
> when they belie her! Lie with her, zounds!, that's
> fulsome! – Handkerchief! confessions! handkerchief!
> – To confess, and be hanged for his labour! First, to be

> hanged, and then to confess: I tremble at it. Nature
> would not invest herself in such shadowing passion
> without some instruction. It is not words that shakes
> me thus. Pish! Noses, ears and lips. Is't possible?
> Confess? handkerchief! O devil!   (IV.1.35–41)

There are a number of points to be made about this breakdown.
Firstly, Othello's fractured sense of self is conveyed through the
lexis and syntax. Previously the hero spoke of himself in the first
and third person (their usage conveyed his nobility and status as
hero); now his use of pronouns 'we', 'they', 'his', 'I', 'me' suggests
insecurity. His use of questions suggests this too. Othello's identity
is threatened because he no longer feels he 'knows' his wife; he
cannot trust her looks and words. There is a terrible irony in the
fact that Othello declares 'It is not words that shake me thus'; the
events of the play and the violence of his outburst here suggest that
words are the cause of Othello's destruction. Note the use of
disjointed prose rather than measured verse: reason has given way
to passion. Othello has also begun to use oaths ('zounds!') which
are associated with Iago, suggesting not only the ensign's power as a
speaker, but also his ability to influence and control the powers of
speech of others. Right at the end of this speech we struggle to make
any sense of Othello's words ('Pish! Noses, ears and lips. Is't
possible? / Confess? handkerchief? O devil!'). These lines suggest
the hero's degradation and degeneration.

From this point on Othello and Desdemona struggle to understand
one another's use of language. The break-up of their marital
harmony is conveyed through the disruption in the lines and
Othello's measured calm gives way to verbal bullying (see
III.4.80–98). This pattern mirrors the disrupted lines of Act III Scene
3 when Iago first started to poison Othello's mind. Desdemona later
says, 'I understand a fury in your words / But not the words'
(IV.2.32–3). By this point he misconstrues everything she says:

> DESDEMONA: Alas, what ignorant sin have I committed?
> OTHELLO: Was this fair paper, this most goodly book
>   Made to write 'whore' upon? ... What, committed!
>   Committed! O thou public commoner!
>   (IV.2.71–4)

 CHECK THE FILM

The Hollywood
retelling of *Othello*,
O (2001) is set in an
American private
high school, where
the lead – Ovin – is
a gifted black
basketball player.
The Desdemona
figure is the
principal's daughter.
The director claimed
that he wanted to
use Shakespeare's
play to 'draw
attention to the
violence that occurs
in American high
schools'.

Eventually, unable to comprehend his wife's honesty, failing to see that her words should be taken at face value, Othello smothers and silences Desdemona. When confronted with the truth he then recovers, returning to the majestic idiom of his earlier speeches at the end of Act V. His final speech echoes his first speech to the senate, but Othello no longer speaks of himself as a worthy hero only. Now he compares himself to 'the base Indian' and 'the circumcised dog' (V.2.345 and 353), his words and syntax recall former glories, but also point towards the 'bloody period' of the hero's death (V.2.354).

Language is the source of Iago's power too, but his characteristic idiom is very different. It is full of compounds, colloquialisms and oaths, befitting a bluff soldier. But Iago's use of language is more complicated than this. We quickly notice that the villain slips between prose and verse, adapting his style to suit his different audiences and purposes. The blunt, persuasive and lucid prose of his exchanges with Roderigo conveys Iago's base nature, but the ensign also makes use of a loftier style too, as in his parody of Othello's idiom in Act III Scene 3 (lines 465–72). This speech is an example of Iago's power: he can manipulate his style effortlessly. Most worryingly for the audience, Othello begins to use the villain's base idiom when he decides to revenge himself on Desdemona, showing his lack of judgement and Iago's increasing authority over him. When he adopts Iago's style and begins to eavesdrop (Iago might be seen as an eavesdropper when he speaks in asides) Othello shows that he has become 'well tun'd' with the wrong character. Iago's heavy use of asides also reveals his cunning, destructive power; he is able to not only direct but also to comment on the action of the play. His use of soliloquies reinforces his power. Elizabethan and Jacobean dramatists used this artificial theatrical convention to evoke the inwardness of their characters, to show what they think and feel. Soliloquies are also used to convey information and for particular dramatic effect. In *Othello* the evil ensign speaks his soliloquies first (Othello's soliloquies occur towards the end of the play), drawing the audience in as he outlines his intentions and ideas. Because we know exactly what his plans are, we might feel that Shakespeare forces us to collude with the villain in some way: Iago is so clever, such an impressive actor. Iago's soliloquies and

CONTEXT

A soliloquy is a dramatic convention that allows a character to speak directly to an audience, indicating their motives, feelings and decisions. In *Othello* we are given access to the feelings and motivations of both victim and tormentor, which heightens the intensity of the drama.

asides are also a source of a great deal of the **dramatic irony** of *Othello*, which increases dramatic tension for the audience. Finally, Iago is also able to manipulate his silences, as in Act III Scene 3 when he deliberately introduces '**stops**' (III.3.123) to infuriate and intrigue Othello. By faking a reluctance to talk he gains the opportunity to speak at length. At the end of the play Iago's defiant and deliberate silence can seem suggestive of continued power (the villain refuses to reveal his motives and admit remorse) or power thwarted; he no longer has the ability to sway others with his words and has perhaps been silenced, like his victim Desdemona. It is both ironic and appropriate that Iago is unmasked by his wife, whose silence he has taken for granted and whose powers of speech he has not taken into account.

This discussion of the hero's and villain's contrasting idioms might be extended; each of the characters in Othello has his or her own style. For example, Cassio's speech is gallant and courtly, Emilia's salty and down-to-earth. The different 'voices' and styles in *Othello* are an important part of the play's power to hold and move the audience. Another very important part of the linguistic power of the play is Shakespeare's use of figurative language, the imagery, which is discussed below in **Images and themes**.

QUESTION

How do the settings contribute to your understanding of the play?

DRAMATIC STRUCTURE

There is a narrow focus in *Othello*. There are two principal locations, Venice and Cyprus, but gradually our attention becomes fixed on a single bedroom, creating a feeling of claustrophobia that is unique in Shakespeare's tragedies. The outer world becomes insignificant as the hero becomes monomaniacal, obsessed with a single concern. The use of Venice as a location is significant. At the end of the sixteenth century, dramatists began to use Italy as a suitable location for revenge tragedies; the Italians were thought to be worldly and Venice in particular was associated with everything that was culturally sophisticated; it was a location that suggested power, order and wealth to the audience. At the beginning of the play Othello appears to have succeeded in Venice on its terms; he has gained both power and wealth. But he is also an outsider: different. The play explores what happens to the hero when he is made to feel this difference. It is appropriate that the **Machiavellian** trickster Iago should originate and appear in an Italian setting before being transported to Cyprus. Shakespeare's use of a war with the Turks and the uneasy atmosphere of the garrison town in Cyprus – a 'halfway house' between civilisation and the heathen world – is also dramatically significant. The war isolates the heroine from everything and everyone she knows; similarly, Othello feels his difference and isolation in Cyprus when he is 'Perplexed in the extreme' (V.2.344). Here, in this unfamiliar setting, with the threat of danger lurking, passions are unleashed and order is destroyed. The storm helps to establish and reflect the fear and violence that the characters will feel in Cyprus, while also being a symbol of Othello and Desdemona's love.

QUESTION

How does Shakespeare arouse our feelings of pity in *Othello*?

The sense of claustrophobia is heightened by the fact that there is no subplot in *Othello*. The action of the play focuses very closely on Iago's role and Othello's reactions to his 'reports' (V.2.183). Even the characters who seem to have other 'lives' are closely linked to the married couple in some way; Roderigo's foolish hopes and Cassio's relationship with Bianca provide us with points of comparison with the Othello–Desdemona match. Our sense of claustrophobia is also heightened because we are aware that we are observing a group of characters who exist in a tightly knit social network, where each person has a clearly defined position and role and a view of each other member of the group. Iago threatens the order and harmony of the network because he is able to manipulate the views of the most powerful group member. The single plot intensifies dramatic tension: we are never given a moment's respite to look away from Iago's progress as he pushes Othello towards tragedy.

The structure of the play relies on reversal and repetition. In the first three acts Iago comes to dominate; in Act I he is clearly the underdog, overlooked and perhaps irrelevant except as an escort for the general's wife. In the second act he forms his plans and sets up his revenge, so that in Act III he is able to 'triumph' over Othello. Conversely, Othello is at his most secure in Acts I and II, when he defends and then consummates his marriage. In Act III he struggles to resist the jealousy that threatens to overpower his reason, succumbing to it in Act IV. In Act V Othello sinks further still when he smothers his wife – he becomes what Iago is: a destructive revenger. At the end of the play the tragic protagonist is partially redeemed when he recognises the truth and chooses to destroy himself, while Iago's downfall is assured when he is revealed as a scoundrel.

There are other repetitions in the play that are important. Othello finds himself on trial in Act I and is then placed in a position where he must judge his lieutenant and his wife in subsequent acts. Roderigo is gulled in each conversation he has with Iago, on each occasion getting closer to danger, until he finds himself participating in a plot against Cassio, which proves fatal to him. Desdemona's repeated attempts at pleading for Cassio are increasingly dangerous to the heroine; as he smothers her Othello believes she is weeping for the lieutenant. Repeated words and phrases are important too. Brabantio's bitter words about Desdemona's deception in Act I Scene 3 come back to haunt Othello in Act III Scene 3 (see line 209), while the repetition of 'honest' in relation to Iago is a source of heavy and alarming irony. All the main characters (with the exception of his wife, interestingly) call Iago 'honest' and the ensign makes extensive use of the word himself when gulling his victims; it is as if Shakespeare is showing the ensign's insidious power to 'enmesh 'em all' (II.3.357) through his ability to get his victims to think of and describe him in the same way.

CHECK THE BOOK

For comments about the fifty-two uses of the word 'honest' in the play, see William Empson in John Wain (ed.), *Othello: Casebook*.

Finally, we should also consider the prop that ignites the tragedy: the handkerchief. This trifle becomes loaded with dramatic significance; the whole plot revolves around this object and like the word 'honest', it passes from one character to another. It becomes a symbol of Desdemona's chastity and worthiness as wife, which are abused, as the handkerchief itself is 'abused' when Emilia passes it on to her husband. But it is also a symbol of deception and lack of knowledge; Desdemona is puzzled as to how she lost it, Othello believes she gave it away, Emilia does not know why her husband covets it, Cassio does not know how it came to be in his chamber, Bianca falsely assumes he received it from another sweetheart. Only Iago knows the whole truth about the handkerchief, which is appropriate given the dramatic structure of the play; for four acts he is the only character who fully understands what is happening, because he has set events in motion. Finally, the construction of scenes is also extremely effective in *Othello*. Long scenes of painful exchanges or confrontation are punctuated by short scenes or moments of violence – verbal and physical.

IRONY

There are various types of **irony** in *Othello*, which relies heavily on **dramatic irony** for its effects. There are also examples of situational and verbal irony which help us the understand the action. Iago is the primary source of dramatic irony; he informs us of his intentions, but his victims do not know that they are being manipulated. This puts us in the uncomfortable position of knowing more than the characters, increasing the tension: will Iago succeed in his diabolical designs or will he be discovered? It can be argued that the irony that surrounds Iago and his role forces us to reject the villain. We may marvel at his ingenuity and skill but we cannot approve of him. We become increasingly worried by the verbal irony of repeated references to him as 'honest', just as we are repulsed by the grim and self-conscious irony of some of his utterances. There is considerable irony in the use of the word 'love' in this play too. Note how frequently it is on Iago's lips when he is gulling his victims; this is rather horrible when we consider that Othello and Desdemona's true love is being destroyed by the false and empty love Iago professes. We might also feel that in some ways the joke is on Iago. He thinks that he is a cunning villain, who can arrogantly conceal his true self and remain detached and aloof while all around him 'lose their cool', but is he not driven by passion? His downfall is ironic; Emilia destroys his reputation as an honest man; this is rather appropriate given the fact that the success of Iago's revenge against Othello was reliant on the successful destruction of Desdemona's reputation.

There are other examples of irony that deserve consideration. Othello and Desdemona's situations are ironic. The former falls at the very moment that he feels he has reached the apogee of his success by marrying the '**divine Desdemona**' (II.1.73); when his conception of himself is most secure, he is undermined. He finds that his heroic past counts for nothing: he is forced into the role of '**circumcised dog**' (V.2.353) by the '**inhuman dog**' (V.1.62) Iago. And having been resolutely sure of Desdemona the hero finds himself

CHECK THE FILM
Orson Welles's 1952 version of *Othello* opens imaginatively with Desdemona's funeral prossession, suggesting the tragic inevitability of events.

wondering why he has married, convinced that he has united himself with 'the cunning whore of Venice' (IV.2.91). For her own part, Desdemona expects to consummate her marriage in Cyprus, but her marriage bed is transformed into her deathbed. Othello's conviction that his wife has weak morals is also heartbreakingly ironic; when he doubts Desdemona, the hero reveals his own weakness. Ironically, other characters reveal their weaknesses when they feel they are on the brink of or have achieved success. Iago is brought down just as he has achieved his aims; Cassio gains promotion only to be disgraced for drunken brawling; Roderigo hopes to kill Cassio and supplant him in Desdemona's affections, but is instead murdered by the man who urged him onto the vile deed, a man whose friendship he believed in. This kind of ironic ignorance is repeated in other relationships in *Othello*. None of the characters truly recognises the real honesty or depravity of those they interact with.

THE TIMESCALE OF *OTHELLO*

The theory of a 'double time scheme' in *Othello* dates from the middle of the nineteenth century. There can be no doubt that there are inconsistencies in the way time is presented in *Othello*; it appears that the disintegration of Othello's mind and marriage occurs extremely fast and Iago recognises that he must move quickly if his plots are to remain concealed, but at the same time the characters also make statements that suggest time is moving quite slowly. Let us deal with these references first. In Act III Scene 3 Iago describes Cassio's lustful dream, which we are told occurred 'lately' (III.3.416) when the ensign shared the lieutenant's bed. In Act III Scene 4 Bianca complains to Cassio that he has stayed away from her a week and Othello himself says that he believes Desdemona has committed adultery with Cassio 'A thousand times' (V.2.210). It seems highly unlikely that Lodovico would be sent from Venice to install Cassio as governor within a week of Othello's arrival in Cyprus. These statements which suggest 'long time' are primarily designed to increase the plausibility of Othello's jealousy. But it is also necessary for Shakespeare to present the poisoning of Othello's mind occurring swiftly, without a substantial interval; it would be undramatic if Iago was to loosen his grip on his victim once he has him in his grasp.

> **CONTEXT**
>
> The critic A. C. Bradley coined the terms 'long and short time' to describe the timescale in Othello.

CHECK THE BOOK

For a fuller discussion of time in *Othello* have a look at A. C. Bradley's *Shakespearean Tragedy*.

This brings us to the question of 'short time'. The first act of *Othello* takes place in one night, and then once the characters have arrived in Cyprus (after an interval travelling) time seems to move very swiftly, increasing the sense of claustrophobia and heightening the intensity of the drama. The characters land just before '**this present hour of five**' (II.2.9–10), the wedding celebrations occur that evening, Cassio is cashiered the same night and we see Iago packing Roderigo off to bed at dawn the following morning. On this day Desdemona pleads for Cassio, having met with him earlier in the morning. Iago sees his chance and moves into action immediately. Between Act III Scene 3 and Act IV Scene 1 there might plausibly be a short interval, but thereafter there can be no break until the curtain falls at the end of Act V. It is this relentlessness that grips us in the theatre, where we do not notice the inconsistencies. It might also be argued that this insistence on 'short time' is a deliberate theatrical decision. Perhaps Shakespeare uses his time scheme to show us how powerful and unreasonable jealousy is; we know that Desdemona has not had the opportunity to commit adultery, and yet her husband becomes convinced she has betrayed him. 'Short time' also favours the dramatist Iago: is *Othello* perhaps a self-reflexive text in which the dramatist colludes with his villain?

IMAGERY

The purpose of Shakespeare's use of imagery in *Othello* is to establish the dramatic atmosphere of the play. It also informs our understanding of characters and events. **Figurative** language and linguistic patterns can help to reinforce the themes and ideas that the dramatist wishes to explore. Some key images are discussed below.

POISONING

There are a number of images of poisoning, which we come to associate with Iago and his methods of manipulation. In Act I Scene 1 the ensign says that he wants to '**poison his** [Brabantio's] **delight**' (I.1.68) so that he can make trouble for Othello. In the following act we learn that Iago's jealousy of the Moor is so strong that it '**Doth like a poisonous mineral gnaw my inwards**' (II.1.295); so the ensign resolves to '**pour this pestilence into his ear**' (II.3.351) and destroy

Othello's 'sweet sleep' (II.3.335). These references to poison are appropriate to Iago, whose actions are swift, insidious and deadly. Iago relishes the pain he causes, as we can see from his description of his methods in Act III Scene 3:

> Dangerous conceits are in their natures poisons
> Which at the first are scarce found to distaste
> But with a little act upon the blood
> Burn like the mines of sulphur.   (III.3.329–32)

In the same scene Othello describes how he feels tortured by jealousy, using images that recall Iago's words, 'If there be cords or knives, / Poison, or fire, or suffocating streams, / I'll not endure it. Would I were satisfied!' (III.3.391–3). The most chilling reference to poison comes in Act IV Scene 1 when Othello decides to murder Desdemona:

> OTHELLO: Get me some poison, Iago, this night. I'll
> not expostulate with her, lest her body and beauty
> unprovide my mind again. This night, Iago.
> IAGO: Do it not with poison, strangle her in her bed –
> even the bed that she hath contaminated.   (IV.1.201–5)

His mind poisoned with foul thoughts, the hero now seeks to kill his wife in the bed that he thinks she has contaminated, poisoned with her lust. It is particularly ghastly that the real poisoner (Iago) suggests the method of killing Desdemona.

HELL AND THE DEVIL

Iago is also associated with images of hell and the devil. He forges the link himself at the end of his soliloquy in Act I Scene 3. Outlining his evil intentions he says, 'Hell and night / Must bring this monstrous birth to the world's light' (I.3.402–3). Later there is the **oxymoron**, 'Divinity of hell!' followed by these lines:

> When devils will their blackest sins put on
> They do suggest at first with heavenly shows
> As I do now   (II.3.345–8)

www. CHECK THE NET
For information on themes, motifs, imagery and symbols go to **www.sparknotes.com/shakespeare/othello**.

There is delight in these lines, a revelling in evil and deception. Iago also describes Othello as 'a devil' (I.1.90), but in this context this seems to be a racial slur rather than a comment on Othello's character; elsewhere the ensign comments on the Moor's natural goodness, which makes his work easier. Iago's hellish designs succeed in making Othello see Desdemona as devilish. He makes a 'sacred vow' (III.3.464) to wreak vengeance on her 'by yond marble heaven' (III.3.463), convincing himself that she is damned and must be stopped in her life of sin. In Act IV Scene 2 Othello attempts to wring an admission of guilt from Desdemona:

> Come, swear it, damn thyself,
> Lest, being like one of heaven, the devils themselves
> Should fear to seize thee   (IV.2.36–8)

In this image we see the enormity of Desdemona's crime from Othello's point of view. As he leaves in disgust, having failed to secure the confession he sought, Othello turns to Emilia and accuses her too; she 'keeps the gates of hell' for his wife (IV.2.94). Emilia turns these words on Othello in the final scene when she discovers Desdemona's murder; 'thou art a devil' she rages, 'the blacker devil' (V.2.131 and 129). But it is of course Iago who is revealed as the true devil in this scene, where he is rightfully described as a 'demi-devil' and 'hellish villain' (V.2.298 and 366).

ANIMALS AND INSECTS

There are numerous references to animals and insects which chart Othello's downfall. In Iago's mouth this imagery is reductive and negative. Several images suggest how much the villain despises his victims. In Act I Scene 1 he sets out with Roderigo to 'Plague him [Brabantio] with flies' (I.1.70). When he describes Othello's match with Desdemona he uses crude animal imagery, 'an old black ram / Is tupping your white ewe' he informs the senator (I.1.87–8); his daughter has been 'covered' with 'a Barbary horse' (I.1.110); the couple are 'making the beast with two backs' (I.1.115). Othello is an object of scorn too. Iago is confident that the general will 'tenderly be led by th'nose / As asses are' (I.2 400–1), and made 'egregiously an ass' (II.1.307). He is sure that Cassio can be humiliated too;

'With as little a web as this will I ensnare as great a fly as Cassio' (II.1.168–9) he gloats.

Othello is infected by this imagery and begins to speak in the same terms. But the animal imagery in Othello's speeches reveals the hero's misery, rather than sneering triumph. In Act III Scene 3 he says:

> I had rather be a toad
> And live upon this vapour of a dungeon
> Than keep a corner in a thing I love
> For others' uses.   (III.3.274–7)

This image is repeated in Act IV Scene 2 when Othello describes his sorrow at 'losing' the innocent Desdemona he loved so much:

> But there where I have garnered up my heart,
> Where either I must live or bear no life,
> The fountain from which my current runs
> Or else dries up – to be discarded thence!
> Or keep it as a cistern for foul toads
> To knot and gender in!   (IV.2.58–63)

The hero is mortified by corruption. Iago keeps Othello on the rack with images of bestial lust; when the Moor demands proof of his suspicions he replies sharply:

> What shall I say? where's satisfaction?
> It is impossible you should see this
> Were they as prime as goats, as hot as monkeys,
> As salt as wolves in pride;   (III.3.404–7)

We know that Othello has lost all power of reason and can no longer fight off the terrible images of lust his imagination has been polluted with when he himself yelps 'Goats and monkeys!' in Act IV Scene 1 (IV.1.263). He has become the 'horned man', the 'monster, and a beast' he described earlier in the same scene (IV.1.62). It is horribly ironic that Desdemona, who, we are informed could 'sing the savageness out of a bear' (IV.1.186) cannot convince her husband that his suspicions are false.

QUESTION

Do you agree with Othello's assessment of himself as a 'monster'?

QUESTION

Why is it
important to the
play's tragic
situation that
Othello, Iago and
Cassio are
soldiers?

THE SEA AND MILITARY HEROISM

In stark contrast to the imagery associated with Iago, the imagery
commonly associated with the noble Othello of the first half of the
play is suggestive of power and bravery. Images of the sea and
military heroism abound. Othello describes his illustrious career
with dignity in Act I Scene 3 (see lines 82–90 and 129–46).
Desdemona echoes him when she says:

> My downright violence and scorn of fortunes
> May trumpet to the world. My heart's subdued
> Even to the very quality of my lord: (I.3.250–2)

By using the terminology of war to describe her love we see that the
heroine is 'well tun'd' (II.1.198) with her husband; it is fitting then
that he describes her as his 'fair warrior' (II.1.179). Later, when
Othello feels his marital harmony has been destroyed we sense how
deeply he feels Desdemona's supposed betrayal as he eggs himself
on to revenge:

> Like to the Pontic sea
> Whose icy current and compulsive course
> Ne'er feels retiring ebb but keeps due on
> To the Propontic and the Hellespont:
> Even so my bloody thoughts with violent pace
> Shall ne'er look back, ne'er ebb to humble love   (III.3.456–61)

The imagery here suggests the violence to come, violence that has
always been implicit in the sea and military imagery associated with
Othello. As he prepares to take his own life Othello again refers to
his military career, but also recognises that he has reached 'my
journey's end, here is my butt / And very sea-mark of my utmost sail'
(V.2.269–6), This final image of the sea is appropriately poignant. By
reverting to the noble imagery associated with him earlier in the play
the hero is able to raise himself again in our esteem.

BLACK AND WHITE

References to black and white are important. There are also images
of light and darkness, heaven and hell (see **Imagery**). Clearly these
images are all related to the central paradox in the play; Othello

who is 'far more fair than black' (I.3.291) is the virtuous, noble man, while his white ensign proves to be a devilish creature with a truly black soul. When Iago blackens Desdemona's character, Othello feels his honour is threatened; he expresses his dismay by referring to his own blackness in a negative way. Up to this point Othello has been proud of his race and secure in his love ('she had eyes, and chose me' he says at III.3.192, suggesting that his colour was irrelevant). Now we sense that the 'black' (in the sense of angry, violent) Othello will supersede the 'fair' Othello:

> I'll have some proof. Her name, that was as fresh
> As Dian's visage, is now begrimed and black
> As mine own face   (III.3.389–91)

We might feel that these lines describe Othello's regret at the corruption of his imagination by Iago; he no longer has a 'fresh' name, instead his mind – as well as his name – is 'begrimed', just as Desdemona's name has been besmirched. Later in the same scene Othello calls for assistance with his revenge, 'Arise, black vengeance, from thy hollow cell' (III.3.450). Here he seems to link himself to hell and darkness, even though he also feels that he is serving heaven by making 'a sacrifice' (V.2.65) of Desdemona. The confusion suggested by these images is appropriate; the hero is pulled in two directions for much of the play, wanting to believe that his 'fair warrior' (II.1.179) is honest, while also believing that she is damned. Desdemona is associated with images of light, divinity and perfection throughout the play. The final metapho Othello uses to speak of her suggests her purity and preciousness; she is 'a pearl' (V.2.345) he threw away like a 'base Indian' (V.2.345). When he stood over her preparing to kill her Othello still could not quite believe that she was false; the metaphor 'Put out the light, and then put out the light' (V.2.7) expresses this idea eloquently. As discussed above, Iago is most often linked to darkness and devils. The drama of the play occurs as Othello moves away from the light of Desdemona's love towards the darkness of Iago and his world view, becoming a black villain in the process. Note how many of the key scenes or events occur at night. It might also be argued that we associate Othello the Moor with darkness from the very beginning of the play; his first entrance occurs at night, and his final act, the

QUESTION

Is Othello 'far more fair than black'?

murder of Desdemona, also occurs at night. Has the Moor in some sense fulfilled his tragic destiny when he snuffs out the light on Desdemona (whose name suggests doom) and himself?

THEMES

JEALOUSY

The imagery associated with the central theme jealousy suggests the destructive, terrifying and perhaps unnatural qualities of this emotion. It is 'the green-eyed monster, which doth mock / The meat it feeds on' (III.3.168–9), 'a monster / Begot upon itself, born on itself' (III.4.161–2). There is a strong sense of devouring and being devoured in these images, which fits in with Iago's description of Othello as being 'eaten up with passion'. These lines suggest the exact quality of Othello's monumental jealousy; once he becomes convinced that his wife is unfaithful, his jealousy does indeed feed itself, leading the hero to behave monstrously. Jealousy is also deeply humiliating in *Othello*; Iago is correct when he says that it is 'A passion most unsuiting such a man' as the noble Moor of Venice (IV.1.78).

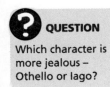

QUESTION

Which character is more jealous – Othello or Iago?

Let us look at Shakespeare's exploration of jealousy more closely. There are three examples of jealousy that shed light on the subject: Iago's personal and professional jealousy, which is linked to feelings of envy and sets events in motion; Bianca's suspicions, which mirror Othello's closely; and the Moor's towering jealousy, which propels him towards tragedy. Iago says that hatred and jealousy gnaw at his inwards like poison; his aim is to make Othello and Cassio suffer as he suffers because he fears he has been cuckolded. We can never be sure that Iago's suspicions are true (Emilia denies that they are) but we feel that the ensign uses jealousy to rationalise his devilment. Like Othello and Bianca, his suspicions are groundless. Has jealousy perhaps turned Iago into a villain? Unlike Othello, however, Iago is cool and calculating when he chooses to act on his suspicions; jealousy follows on naturally from hatred in his **characterisation**.

Does Othello's insistence on proof suggest that this jealous husband is a nobler man? Certainly we feel that his sexual jealousy is motivated by affection rather than hatred; in this example the 'green-ey'd monster' (III.3.169) seems to be the 'flipside' of boundless love. What Othello shares with Iago is covetousness; both men feel jealous because they have lost possession of something that they held dear, just as Bianca fears that she has lost Cassio's heart to a new lover. Because Desdemona and Emilia insist that they have done nothing to give their husbands cause to be jealous, we cannot see jealousy except as a negative emotion. We agree with Emilia's assessment that it is monstrous; it destroys love, honour and nobility in those it afflicts. It makes both male protagonists murderous and violent: it is a form of tyranny. It also seems that it is the nature of jealousy not to be satisfied. Iago continues plotting against Cassio after he has disgraced him and is not content with disturbing Othello's peace of mind, he must continue until Desdemona is dead. Finally, it might be argued that we also come to view jealousy as ridiculous as well as terrifying and chaotic. Iago's motives for revenge are surely inadequate and the handkerchief absurdly comes to symbolise Desdemona's virtue.

QUESTION

What destroys Othello's marriage?

MEN AND WOMEN

Various ideas are explored through same sex and male–female relationships in *Othello*; sex and violence, love and hate, honour and dishonesty, loyalty and betrayal, trust and suspicion. Power is also a key factor in all the relationships portrayed. To begin with we are presented with a picture of powerful womanhood; a daughter has deceived her father and asserted her independence from patriarchy by choosing her own husband. The example set by Desdemona shows that male–female relationships are to be locus of conflict in this play; they are about opposition and power. Throughout the play we see further power struggles between couples and friends; Iago vies with Desdemona for Othello's ear, Desdemona and Emilia defend themselves against their husbands' suspicions, Bianca works hard to assert her rights as Cassio's mistress. Initially, Desdemona and Othello stand apart from the other couples in this play because they appear to have an equal relationship; there is no disillusionment or dissatisfaction here. Bianca and Cassio and Emilia and Iago are not happy couplings. The former is clearly an unequal match between a '**customer**' (IV.1.120) who feels a limited ffection and a '**bauble**' (IV.1.134), whose genuine love makes her unhappy. Cassio reveals the limitations of this relationship – which he clearly feels is unworthy in some way – when he tells Bianca to be gone because he would not be seen in her company. Emilia and Iago have a chilling match. Marriage has made Emilia cynical about male–female relationships; she knows she is merely 'food' (III.4.105) for Iago, acceptable until she disobeys him and refuses to be silent, at which point she is dismissed as a 'Villainous whore' (V.2.227). The misogyny of Iago (and Cassio) casts a dark shadow over Othello's relationship with Desdemona, which seems so bright and full of optimism and delight at the start of the play.

Despite their different social, cultural and racial backgrounds the hero and heroine symbolise a meeting of two minds in Acts I and II. He loves her for her feminine grace and sympathy, she loves him for his masculine heroism. Essentially, Othello and Desdemona love each other harmoniously *because of* the differences they perceive in each other. These differences become distorted during the course of the play by an interloper, a man who cannot bear to see two lovers 'well tun'd' (II.1.198). In some ways it is possible to see the Othello–Desdemona–Iago relationship as a kind of love triangle; perhaps the ensign seeks to force Othello to return to the masculine values he embodies as a soldier.

QUESTION

Do you agree that Emilia and Desdemona are too weak and gullible to be convincing?

Let us look more closely at what it is that Iago objects to so strongly when he looks at Othello and Desdemona together. The text suggests that there is something very complicated going on. Iago's responses to the feminine reveal a mixture of fear and loathing. It is possible to argue that part of his contempt for Othello is located in his fear that Desdemona has power; he has been displaced and what's more, Othello married without his knowledge. We know from his sneering references to Desdemona as being the general's 'general' (II.3.310) that he cannot bear the fact that a female now seems to exert power, that he despises Othello for giving into feminine emotions like love. His relationship with Othello becomes a power struggle in which he attempts to assert his false love over Desdemona's true love. He achieves this by denigrating her, by making her voice seem unreliable and his the voice to be believed. This power struggle becomes clearer when we consider the vow he makes at the end of Act III Scene 3. Iago's hatred destroys Othello's love, and leads him to assert his masculine power in an overbearing way. The Moor believes that Desdemona has begun to assert herself sexually in a masculine way; adultery with Cassio means that the duty she said she owed to him has been subverted. We might see the events of Acts IV and V as an attempt by Othello to rein in his wife and reassert his own power over her: we come to associate masculine love with violence. Iago's misogyny triumphs; all the female characters are silenced, their fragile power negated. That they ever had any power in this play is debatable; they are only ever seen in relation to the male characters, who have the power to describe, define and kill them. Even in Act IV Scene 3 when we see Desdemona and Emilia together, the topic of conversation is men and how to interpret them.

But although the women are destroyed and the masculine state reasserts itself, masculine power, values and behaviour are not condoned or affirmed by the events of *Othello*. The masculine hierarchy has lost Desdemona and her valiant husband, who were its jewels, both personally and professionally. Othello's tragedy is that his love, which could have co-existed peacefully with his military career (the state seems to accept this when they allow Othello and Desdemona to go to Cyprus together) is destroyed by the masculine code of one of its basest elements. And finally, it is the women, their characters and actions which are justified. They behave honourably and are vindicated.

RACE AND COLOUR

Strictly speaking, race cannot be considered a theme in the same way that jealousy and love are themes in *Othello*; however, it is impossible to arrive at a satisfactory interpretation of the play, its characters and events without considering the way race and colour are presented. As we have seen above, the wealth of imagery of black and white, light and dark suggests that colour is important in this play (see **Imagery**). It is not possible to define Othello's race and colour exactly; critics have argued about Shakespeare's intentions for his hero; that he is a Negro, that he is Arabian, that he is some other race. A number of critics have also argued that the hero's race is irrelevant; but if this is the case, why did Shakespeare bother to break with dramatic tradition and present a Moorish hero

 CHECK THE BOOK

For comments on the contemporary representation of Africans and blackamoors in the Renaissance, see Virginia Mason Vaughan, *Othello: A Contextual History.*

at all? Before *Othello* black characters in Elizabethan drama were usually villains; the presentation of a noble Moor must mean something. Some commentators suggest that Shakespeare presents a black hero to introduce the idea of difference. Others argue Othello's racial origins make him an outsider. Certainly we might consider the use of a black hero in relation to two key ideas that are explored in the play; dislocation and opposition.

We are presented with at least two opposing views of Othello's blackness. Early in the play positive descriptions come from the Moor himself, who seems proud of his heritage, the Duke of Venice and Desdemona. The fact that Othello has risen to the important and powerful position of general and is accepted as a distinguished member of Venetian society suggests that the state he serves is at least 'colour blind', prepared to see good in foreigners and accept that they have a useful role to play.

CONTEXT

England and Morocco were closely linked in the late sixteenth century through trade. Elizabeth I set up the Barbary Company, and an embassy of Moroccans was received at court in 1600. At the same time, Elizabeth was responsible for a decree that tried to expel foreigners from England. English attitudes to 'foreigners' were clearly contradictory.

But it is noticeable that even Desdemona, who never regrets her marriage and refuses to accept that her love for valiant Othello can ever be tainted, has to explain her choice; she defends her marriage by saying she 'saw Othello's visage in his mind' (I.3.253); in other words, she looks past his colour. Is Shakespeare suggesting that Othello is the exception to the rule that black is usually bad, or urging us to see that racial differences do not matter in affairs of the heart? If this is the case, Desdemona holds a radical point of view; she is probably the only character in the play who does not view miscegenation with anxiety. Do the Duke's words to Brabantio suggest caution? Consider the line, 'your son in law is far more fair than black' (I.3.291). Is this an attempt by the Duke to excuse Othello's blackness? Does this line mean 'try to accept your daughter's marriage because the man she has married is virtuous, even though he is black'? Or is this an example of another white character pleading for racial tolerance?

There is another very negative view of Othello's blackness, which is undermined because we do not respect the speakers, or at least question their judgement. To Iago, Roderigo and Brabantio Othello's colour and racial background – particularly in relation to his marrying a white female – are alarming. Their references to a 'sooty bosom' (I.2.70), 'the thicklips' (I.1.65), and 'an old black ram' (I.1.87) who practises witchcraft in order to subdue a terrified maiden construct a negative stereotype of the hero. These descriptions are inaccurate. The Othello they describe does not exist, although it is possible to argue that the hero begins to display some of the negative aspects of the stereotype when he is persecuted by Iago; he is superstitious (the handkerchief), he is passionate and he does becomes violent. However, many would argue that he shares these characteristics with the white devil who torments him. Ultimately, regardless of the prejudice these characters – and Emilia – show, we will probably respond to Othello's blackness positively, even when the hero himself doubts his attractions. He is more noble and impressive than any of the other male characters in the play and his history is fascinating. We can see why Desdemona chose Othello and appreciate the uniqueness of her choice; is important to remember that the heroine made a very active and positive choice. Othello stresses this when he says 'she had eyes and chose me' (III.3.192); there is no question that the black hero had to force himself on the white heroine and it is also of course Desdemona who insists – publicly – on being allowed to enjoy her marital rights, not her husband. If Othello's colour becomes slightly problematic in the second half of the play it is because Iago's racism is insidious; he destroys the black–white harmony that existed and makes the hero behave in a way that we feel is unnatural for him (Othello finds it almost impossible to reject and destroy Desdemona; for Iago violence comes easily).

So far as dislocation is concerned, critics have argued that the hero's tragedy comes about because he can never be anything except an outsider; he is in an untenable position as a black man serving a white patriarchy. These critics would argue that it is absurd of Othello to expect to carve out a place for himself in his adopted society because its members will never truly accept him. There are other ideas of dislocation to consider too. We might feel that the black hero is dislocated because he marries a white woman, turning his back on his profession to become a lover-husband. Othello becomes further dislocated when he views his own race negatively, giving in to Iago's racism.

CHECK THE BOOK

To see the portrait of the Moorish ambassador to Queen Elizabeth, see the black and white reproduction in either John Russell Brown's Shakespeare: *The Tragedies* or the *Cambridge School Shakespeare* 1992 edition of the play.

CRITICAL HISTORY

Much of the criticism of *Othello* has focused on the two male protagonists and their culpability. Unsurprisingly, there are radically different views of Othello and Iago. Although critics have not dealt so thoroughly with Desdemona's role until more recently, divergent readings of the heroine have also emerged. Race, religion and love have all been considered closely, particularly since 1900. Critics have also explored the tragic vision that Shakespeare presents in this play, comparing *Othello* with the other great tragedies (*King Lear, Hamlet, Macbeth*), which most have considered to be superior to this 'domestic tragedy'. This section offers an overview of some of the key ideas that have been presented in the past 350 years.

EARLY VIEWS

CONTEXT

Thomas Rymer was equally dismissive of the implausible characters: Othello was a 'Jealous Booby', Iago too villainous to be believed, the Venetians despicable, and Desdemona a woman without sense because she married a blackamoor.

Thomas Rymer, one of the play's earliest and most negative critics, produced a detailed commentary on *Othello* in *A Short View of Tragedy* (1693). His views are rather eccentric, but entertaining and thought provoking. Rymer considered the plot untrue to life; he could not believe that soldiers would ever behave as they do in *Othello*. Summing up, Rymer suggested that *Othello* was 'the most lamentable [play] that ever appear'd on any stage. A noble Venetian Lady is to be murdered by our Poet, – in sober sadness, purely for being a Fool', 'the tragical part is plainly none other than a Bloody Farce, without salt or savour'. Rymer was disappointed because the playwright did not provide a satisfactory moral for the audience to take home 'for their use and edification'. He suggested (facetiously) that *Othello* might serve only as 'a warning to good housewives to look well to their linen'.

In stark contrast, Dr Johnson (1765) declared that *Othello* was true to life, and that in this play Shakespeare depicted human nature very skilfully. His response to the hero was largely positive; in Johnson's view Othello was 'magnanimous, artless, and credulous, boundless in his confidence, ardent in his affection, inflexible in his resolution,

and obdurate in his revenge'. He also suggested that the play
provided a 'very useful moral, not to make an unequal match'.
Finally, Johnson praised the construction of *Othello*, which allowed
the drama to unfold with 'scrupulous regularity'.

NINETEENTH-CENTURY VIEWS

Writing at the beginning of the nineteenth century, Coleridge
offered a view of Iago's **characterisation** that has proved to be
extremely influential. He found the villain's evil inscrutable and
argued that Shakespeare presented 'A being next to the devil',
driven by 'motiveless malignity'; in other words, Coleridge suggests
that Iago operates without adequate motivation; he is bad because
he is bad. The critic Hazlitt, whose lectures on Shakespeare and
Elizabethan drama were popular, saw Iago in a similar light,
referring to him as 'an aesthete of evil' and an 'amateur of tragedy'.
Many contemporary critics have taken up these ideas, seeking to
explain Iago's motivation and psychological make-up and
commenting on his skill as a 'dramatist'. Other nineteenth-century
critics shared Rymer's views about Desdemona's marriage to
Othello, suggesting that she must be a strumpet who lacks morals
and self-respect because she chooses to marry a Moor. At the end of
the century Swinburne argued that Othello must be seen as a truly
noble hero, 'the noblest man of man's making'.

> **CONTEXT**
>
> The first black
> actor to play
> Othello was an
> American, Ira
> Aldridge. He
> performed on
> English and
> German stages in
> the 1830s and
> 1840s, but not on
> the American
> stage.

RECENT VIEWS

Two opposing views of the hero and villain have dominated
criticism of *Othello* this century. One school of thought suggests
that Othello is a noble hero who is brought down by a devil, whose
actions cannot be explained satisfactorily. Some who subscribe to
this reading cast Othello as a credulous fool who is out of his depth
among the sophisticated Venetians. Opponents of this view play
down Iago's cunning, describing the villain as a worldly realist who
locates and exploits his general's weak spot; in this reading it is
possible to view Othello as flawed and self-regarding, rather than
inherently noble.

CHECK THE NET

For more information on Bradley and his views, go to **www.clicknotes.com/bradley**.

In 1904 A. C. Bradley presented an overwhelmingly positive analysis of Othello, whom he saw as blameless. For Bradley, Othello was 'the most romantic figure among Shakespeare's heroes ... [he] does not belong to our world'. Bradley's Othello is a man of mystery, exoticism and intense feeling, trustful, open, passionate but self-controlled, 'so noble ... [he] inspires a passion of mingled love and pity' which none of Shakespeare's other heroes is able to inspire. Bradley also commented on Othello's poetic qualities and argued that the newness of his marriage makes his jealousy credible. Iago's methods are also considered to be plausible in this critic's reading of the play. Bradley believed that Othello never falls completely and suggested that at the end of the play we feel 'admiration and love' for the hero, because we exult in the power of 'love and man's inconquerable mind'. Many other commentators have concurred with Bradley's suggestion that love is the central idea in *Othello* and confirmed Othello as one of the greatest lovers in literature; in a number of these readings critics have been also been alarmed by the Moor's total erotic commitment.

Two very influential critics rejected Bradley's analysis of the hero. In these readings Othello emerges as a weak and inadequate figure. T. S. Eliot ('Shakespeare and the Stoicism of Seneca', 1927) accused Othello of self-dramatisation. Focusing on his last speech he says the Moor is guilty of trying to cheer himself up as he attempts to evade reality; for Eliot this speech is a 'terrible exposure of human weakness'. F. R. Leavis ('Diabolic Intellect and the Noble Hero', 1952) also rejected Bradley's reading of Othello's character. He argued that the tragic protagonist was responsible for his own downfall: Iago's role is 'subordinate and merely ancillary'. Leavis claims that Othello has a propensity to jealousy and possesses a weak character, which is sorely tested by marriage; 'the stuff of which he is made begins at once to deteriorate and show itself unfit'. Othello's' love is dismissed; it is 'composed very largely of ignorance of self as well as ignorance of her [Desdemona]'. Othello emerges as ferociously stupid in Leavis's reading. So far as Iago is concerned, Leavis feels that he displays 'a not uncommon kind of grudging malice' and has enough of a grievance to explain his motivation. The Bradley–Leavis debate has continued, with commentators exploring Othello's flaws and nobility and arguing about whether Iago is motiveless evil personified or simply a sour subordinate with petty but adequate motives for revenge. Some critics question whether Iago understands his own motivations. Since the 1950s there have been a number of suggestions that Iago is driven by latent homosexuality. Hazlitt's view of the villain has been extended so that Iago is now considered an example of the typical stage **Machiavel** who 'personifies rationality, self-interest, hypocrisy, cunning, expediency and efficient "policie"', he is an 'amoral artist' who seeks to fashion a world in his own image (Leah Scragg, 'Iago – vice or devil?' *Shakespeare Survey 21*, 1968).

Desdemona has received a good deal of critical attention during this century. Some commentators suggest she is a goddess and a saint, others see her as a representative of goodness and purity, whose self-control and innocence are praiseworthy. Many critics have commented on her commitment to love and loving. A different view of Desdemona and what she represents has emerged in recent years; **feminist** and **new historicist** critics have examined her character in relation to the society she moves in and its value systems. Marilyn French (*Shakespeare's Division of Experience*, Abacus, 1982) explores the masculine and misogynistic value system at work in *Othello*. Inspite of her masculine assertiveness in choosing her own husband, French suggests Desdemona 'accepts her culture's dictum that she must be obedient to males' and is 'self-denying in the extreme' when she dies. French also comments on the feminine values that she feels Othello, Emilia, Cassio and Roderigo subscribe to, which are destroyed by Iago, whose 'ordinary wisdom of the male world' comes to dominate. Lisa Jardine (*Still Harping on Daughters*, 1983) suggests that the stage world of Jacobean drama is wholly masculine and argues that there is only a male viewpoint on offer. Jardine asserts the view that Desdemona proves to be 'too-knowing, too-independent', that 'The shadow of sexual frailty hovers over' her throughout the play. Because of her waywardness she is punished by patriarchy, which gives women licence to scold but then revokes that licence; ultimately, Jardine suggests Desdemona is a patient Griselda, 'glorious in her resignation in the face of husbandly chastisement', she shows 'exemplary passivity in adversity' and becomes a stereotype of female passivity.

 CHECK THE FILM

Many famous twentieth-century film and stage productions, including Orson Welles' and Laurence Olivier's, sought to emphasise Desdemona's innocence and purity, and her difference from Othello, by portraying her as a light-skinned blonde.

Commenting on the violence against female characters in drama of this period, Leonard Tennenhouse (*Power on Display*, 1986) asserts the view that 'Jacobean tragedies offer up their scenes of excessive punishment as if mutilating the female could somehow correct political corruption. The female in question may be completely innocent, her torture gratuitous, yet in play after play she demands her own death or else claims responsibility for her murder.' Tennenhouse explores the way in which women are cast as monsters in Jacobean tragedy, primarily because of their sexuality. He also suggests that male–female relationships in Jacobean drama are always political. In *Othello* he sees Desdemona's smothering as an example of the silencing of the female political voice.

In *Gender, Race, Renaissance Drama* (1987) Ania Loomba extends these discussions of gender and politics to include race. For her, this play is about the very complex relationship between a black man, a white woman and the state. Like the critics mentioned above Loomba focuses on the structures of oppression in Renaissance texts and explores the radical instability and contradictions they throw up. For Loomba, women and blacks exist as 'the other' in this play. Loomba argues that Othello has a split consciousness and is 'a near schizophrenic hero'; his final speech 'graphically portrays the split – he becomes simultaneously the Christian and the Infidel, the Venetian and the Turk, the keeper of the state and its opponent'. She also argues that 'Othello's colour and gender make him occupy contradictory positions in relation to power'. Othello is an honorary white at the beginning of the play but becomes a 'total outsider', marginalised from society and its ideology by his relationship with Desdemona, which ruptures his 'precarious entry into the white world' and 'catalyses the contradictions in Othello's self-conception'. Loomba suggests that Desdemona 'passes from being his ally who would guarantee his white status to becoming his sexual and racial "other"' when her husband sees her as an adulteress. Essentially, for this critic, the central conflict in *Othello* is 'between the racism of a white patriarchy and the threat posed to it by both a black man and a white woman'. Class and gender relations are invaded by race. Finally, Loomba insists that *Othello* 'should not be read as a patriarchal, authoritative and racist spectacle, nor as a show of female or black superiority'; instead the

CONTEXT

When Paul Robeson, a highly regarded Othello, kissed the actress playing Desdemona in a 1943 Broadway production, it was the first time that a black actor had kissed a white actress in a major theatre.

play should be used to 'examine and dismantle the racism and
sexism' of **hegemonic** ideologies.

Several twentieth-century critics have been preoccupied by the
Christianity of Othello the character and *Othello* the play. Many
have noted the Christian signification of certain speeches (e.g. V.2.33
and V.2.24). Othello has been compared to Job, Judas and Adam;
Desdemona with Christ and Iago with Satan. Some critics suggest
that Othello is damned when he commits suicide because he has
sinned against God's law. Othello is also accused of other soul
destroying sins; murder, despair and entering into a compact with
the devil (Iago). Other critics suggest that *Othello* simply affirms a
morality that is consistent with Christianity; it presents a positive
view of love and faith, shows us that vengeance is wicked, pride
dangerous and frowns on the malice and destructiveness of jealousy
and malice.

Finally, there has been a number of close analyses of the language of
Othello; three much-admired texts which are worth looking at in
full are G. Wilson-Knight's, 'The *Othello* Music' (1930) from *The
Wheel of Fire* (Knight also looks at the morality of the hero),
William Empson's 'Honest in Othello' (from *The Structure of
Complex Words*, Chatto & Windus, 1951) in which the author
argues that there are a number of ways of interpreting the use of this
very perplexing word and R. B. Heilman's *Magic in the Web* (1956),
a very thorough exploration of the language of *Othello*.

 **CHECK
THE NET**
For images of past
stage and film
productions of the
play, and a link to
artworks related to
Othello go to
**www.meredith.
edu** – search for
'*Othello*'.

PART FIVE

BACKGROUND

WILLIAM SHAKESPEARE'S LIFE

There are no personal records of Shakespeare's life. Official documents and occasional references to him by contemporary dramatists enable us to draw the main outline of his public life, but his private life remains hidden. Although not at all unusual for a writer of his time, this lack of first-hand evidence has tempted many to read his plays as personal records and to look in them for clues to Shakespeare's character and convictions. The results are unconvincing, partly because Renaissance art was not subjective or designed primarily to express its creator's personality, and partly because the drama of any period is very difficult to read biographically. Except when plays are written by committed dramatists to promote social or political causes (as by Shaw or Brecht), it is all but impossible to decide who amongst the variety of fictional characters in a drama represents the dramatist, or which of the various and often conflicting points of view expressed is authorial.

What we do know can be quickly summarised. Shakespeare was born into a well-to-do family in the market town of Stratford-upon-Avon in Warwickshire, where he was baptised, in Holy Trinity Church, on 26 April 1564. His father, John Shakespeare, was a prosperous glover and leather merchant who became a person of some importance in the town: in 1565 he was elected an alderman of the town, and in 1568 he became high bailiff (or mayor) of Stratford. In 1557 he had married Mary Arden. Their third child (of eight) and eldest son, William, learned to read and write at the primary (or 'petty') school in Stratford and then, it seems probable, attended the local grammar school, where he would have studied Latin, history, logic and rhetoric. In November 1582 William, then aged eighteen, married Anne Hathaway, who was twenty-six years old. They had a daughter, Susanna, in May 1583, and twins, Hamnet and Judith, in 1585.

CHECK THE BOOK

There are a number of biographies of Shakespeare – many of them very speculative – but the most authoritative is still Samuel Schoenbaum's *Shakespeare: A Documentary Life* (1975).

Shakespeare next appears in the historical record in 1592 when he is mentioned as a London actor and playwright in a pamphlet by the dramatist Robert Greene. These 'lost years' 1585–92 have been the subject of much speculation, but how they were occupied remains as much a mystery as when Shakespeare left Stratford, and why. In his pamphlet, *Greene's Groatsworth of Wit*, Greene expresses to his fellow dramatists his outrage that the 'upstart crow' Shakespeare has the impudence to believe he 'is as well able to bombast out a blank verse as the best of you'. To have aroused this hostility from a rival, Shakespeare must, by 1592, have been long enough in London to have made a name for himself as a playwright. We may conjecture that he had left Stratford in 1586 or 1587.

During the next twenty years, Shakespeare continued to live in London, regularly visiting his wife and family in Stratford. He continued to act, but his chief fame was as a dramatist. From 1594 he wrote exclusively for the Lord Chamberlain's Men, which rapidly became the leading dramatic company and from 1603 enjoyed the patronage of James I as the King's Men. His plays were extremely popular and he became a shareholder in his theatre company. He was able to buy lands around Stratford and a large house in the town, to which he retired about 1611. He died there on 23 April 1616 and was buried in Holy Trinity Church on 25 April.

SHAKESPEARE'S DRAMATIC CAREER

Between the late 1580s and 1613 Shakespeare wrote thirty-seven plays, and contributed to some by other dramatists. This was by no means an exceptional number for a professional playwright of the times. The exact date of the composition of individual plays is a matter of debate –the date of first performance is known for only a few plays – but the broad outlines of Shakespeare's dramatic career have been established. He began in the late 1580s and early 1590s by rewriting earlier plays and working with plotlines inspired by the Classics. He concentrated on comedies (such as *The Comedy of Errors*, 1590–4, which derived from the Latin playwright Plautus) and plays dealing with English history (such as the three parts of *Henry VI*, 1589–92), though he also tried his hand at bloodthirsty revenge tragedy (*Titus Andronicus*, 1592–3, indebted to both Ovid and Seneca). During the 1590s Shakespeare developed his expertise

 CHECK THE NET
You can read Shakespeare's will in his own handwriting – and in modern transcription – online at the Public Records Office: **http://www.pro. gov.uk/ virtualmuseum** and search for 'Shakespeare'.

CHECK THE FILM

There are lots of anachronisms and inaccuracies in *Shakespeare in Love* (1998) – that's half the fun of it – but its depiction of the hand-to-mouth world of the commercial theatre has something of the energy and edginess from which Shakespeare drew his artistic power.

CONTEXT

A quarto is a small format book, roughly equivalent to a modern paperback. Play texts in quarto form typically cost sixpence, as opposed to the cost of going to the theatre at a penny.

in these kinds of plays to write comic masterpieces such as *A Midsummer Night's Dream* (1594–5) and *As You Like It* (1599–1600) and history plays such as *Henry IV* (1596–8) and *Henry V* (1598–9).

As the new century begins a new note is detectable. Plays such as *Troilus and Cressida* (1601–2) and *Measure for Measure* (1603–4), poised between comedy and tragedy, evoke complex responses. Because of their generic uncertainty and ambivalent tone such works are sometimes referred to as 'problem plays', but it is tragedy which comes to dominate the extraordinary sequence of masterpieces: *Hamlet* (1600–1), *Othello* (1602–4), *King Lear* (1605–6), *Macbeth* (1605–6) and *Antony and Cleopatra* (1606).

In the last years of his dramatic career, Shakespeare wrote a group of plays of a quite different kind. These 'romances', as they are often called, are in many ways the most remarkable of all his plays. The group comprises *Pericles* (1608), *Cymbeline* (1609–11), *The Winter's Tale* (1610–11) and *The Tempest* (1610–11). These plays (particularly *Cymbeline*) reprise many of the situations and themes of the earlier dramas but in fantastical and exotic dramatic designs which, set in distant lands, covering large tracts of time and involving music, mime, dance and tableaux, have something of the qualities of masques and pageants. The situations which in the tragedies had led to disaster are here resolved: the great theme is restoration and reconciliation. Where in the tragedies Ophelia, Desdemona and Cordelia die, the daughters of these plays – Marina, Imogen, Perdita, Miranda – survive and are reunited with their parents and lovers.

THE TEXTS OF SHAKESPEARE'S PLAYS

Nineteen of Shakespeare's plays were printed during his lifetime in what are called 'quartos': books, each containing one play, and made up of sheets of paper each folded twice to make four leaves. Shakespeare, however, did not supervise their publication. This was not unusual. When a playwright sold a play to a dramatic company he sold his rights in it: copyright belonged to whoever had possession of an actual copy of the text, and consequently authors had no control over what happened to their work. Anyone who could get hold of the text of a play might publish it if they wished. Hence, what found its way into print might be the author's copy, but it might be an actor's copy or prompt copy, perhaps cut or altered for performance; sometimes actors (or even members of the audience) might publish what they could remember of the text. Printers, working without the benefit of the author's oversight, introduced their own errors, through misreading the manuscript for example, and by 'correcting' what seemed to them not to make sense.

In 1623 John Heminges and Henry Condell, two actors in Shakespeare's company, collected together texts of thirty-six of Shakespeare's plays (*Pericles* was omitted) and published them in a large folio (a book in which each sheet of paper is folded once in half, to give two leaves). This, the First Folio, was followed by later editions in 1632, 1663 and 1685. Despite its appearance of authority, however, the texts in the First Folio still present many difficulties, for there are printing errors and confused passages in the plays, and its texts often differ significantly from those of the earlier quartos, when these exist.

Shakespeare's texts have, then, been through a number of intermediaries. We do not have the playwright's authority for any of his plays, and hence we cannot know exactly what it was that he wrote. Bibliographers, textual critics and editors have spent a great deal of effort on endeavouring to get behind the errors, uncertainties and contradictions in the available texts to recover the plays as Shakespeare originally wrote them. What we read is the result of these efforts. Modern texts are what editors have constructed from the available evidence: they correspond to no sixteenth- or seventeenth-century editions, and to no early performance of a Shakespeare play. Furthermore, these composite texts differ from each other, for different editors read the early texts differently and come to different conclusions. A Shakespeare text is an unstable and a contrived thing.

Often, of course, its judgements embody, if not the personal prejudices of the editor, then the cultural preferences of the time in which he or she was working. Growing awareness of this has led

---

CONTEXT

Plays were not considered as serious literature in this period: when, in 1612, Sir Thomas Bodley was setting up his library in Oxford he instructed his staff not to buy any drama for the collection: 'haply [perhaps] some plays may be worthy the keeping, but hardly one in forty.'

 CHECK THE NET

You can find out more about the earliest editions of Shakespeare at the University of Pensylvannia's ERIC site: **http://oldsite. library.upenn.edu/ etext/collections/ furness/eric/eric. html**.

recent scholars to distrust the whole editorial enterprise and to repudiate the attempt to construct a 'perfect' text. Stanley Wells and Gary Taylor, the editors of the Oxford edition of *The Complete Works* (1988), point out that almost certainly the texts of Shakespeare's plays were altered in performance, and from one performance to another, so that there may never have been a single version. They note, too, that Shakespeare probably revised and rewrote some plays. They do not claim to print a definitive text of any play, but prefer what seems to them the 'more theatrical' version, and when there is a great difference between available versions, as with *King Lear*, they print two texts.

SHAKESPEARE AND THE ENGLISH RENAISSANCE

Shakespeare arrived in London at the very time that the Elizabethan period was poised to become the 'golden age' of English literature. Although Elizabeth reigned as queen from 1558 to 1603, the term 'Elizabethan' is used very loosely in a literary sense to refer to the period 1580 to 1625, when the great works of the age were produced. (Sometimes the later part of this period is distinguished as 'Jacobean', from the Latin form of the name of the king who succeeded Elizabeth, James I of England and VI of Scotland, who reigned from 1603 to 1625.) The poet Edmund Spenser heralded this new age with his pastoral poem *The Shepheardes Calender* (1579), and in his essay *An Apologie for Poetrie* (written about 1580, although not published until 1595) his friend Sir Philip Sidney championed the imaginative power of the 'speaking picture of poesy', famously declaring that 'Nature never set forth the earth in so rich a tapestry as divers poets have done ... Her world is brazen, the poet's only deliver a golden'.

CHECK THE NET

You can consult texts by Spenser and Sidney, and other contemporaries of Shakespeare , at Renascence Editions **http://www. uoregon.edu/ ~rbear/ren.htm**.

Spenser and Sidney were part of that rejuvenating movement in European culture which since the nineteenth century has been known by the term 'Renaissance'. Meaning literally 'rebirth' it denotes a revival and redirection of artistic and intellectual endeavour which began in Italy in the fourteenth century with the poetry of Petrarch. It spread gradually northwards across Europe, and is first detectable in England in the early sixteenth century in the writings of the scholar and statesman Sir Thomas More and in the poetry of Sir Thomas Wyatt and Henry Howard, Earl of Surrey. Its keynote was a curiosity in thought which challenged old assumptions and traditions. To the innovative spirit of the Renaissance, the preceding ages appeared dully unoriginal and conformist.

That spirit was fuelled by the rediscovery of many Classical texts and the culture of Greece and Rome. This fostered a confidence in human reason and in human potential which, in every sphere, challenged old convictions. The discovery of America and its peoples (Columbus had sailed in 1492) demonstrated that the world was a larger and stranger place than had been thought. The cosmological speculation of Copernicus (later confirmed by Galileo) that the sun, not the earth was the centre of our planetary system challenged the centuries-old belief that the earth and human beings were at the centre of the cosmos. The pragmatic political philosophy of Machiavelli seemed to cut politics free from its traditional link with morality by permitting to statesmen any means that secured the desired end. And the religious movements we know collectively as the Reformation broke with the Church of Rome and set the individual conscience, not ecclesiastical authority, at the centre of the religious life. Nothing, it seemed, was beyond questioning, nothing impossible.

Shakespeare's drama is innovative and challenging in exactly the way of the Renaissance. It examines and questions the beliefs, assumptions and politics upon which Elizabethan society was founded. And although the plays always conclude in a restoration of order and stability, many critics are inclined to argue that their imaginative energy goes into subverting, rather than reinforcing, traditional values. Frequently, figures of authority are undercut by some comic or parodic figure: against the Duke in *Measure for Measure* is set Lucio; against Prospero in *The Tempest*, Caliban; against Henry IV, Falstaff. Despairing, critical, dissident, disillusioned, unbalanced, rebellious, mocking voices are repeatedly to be heard in the plays, rejecting, resenting, defying the established order. They belong always to marginal, socially unacceptable figures, 'licensed', as it were, by their situations to say what would be unacceptable from socially privileged or responsible citizens. The

CHECK THE NET

The Luminarium site has links to a wide range of historical information on sixteenth-century topics including astronomy, medicine, economics and technology: **http://www.luminarium.org**.

question is: are such characters given these views to discredit them, or were they the only ones through whom a voice could be given to radical and dissident ideas? Was Shakespeare a conservative or a revolutionary?

Renaissance culture was intensely nationalistic. With the break-up of the internationalism of the Middle Ages the evolving nation states which still mark the map of Europe began for the first time to acquire distinctive cultural identities. There was intense rivalry among them as they sought to achieve, in their own vernacular languages, a culture that could equal that of Greece and Rome. Spenser's great allegorical epic poem *The Faerie Queene*, which began to appear from 1590, celebrated Elizabeth and was intended to outdo the poetic achievements of France and Italy and to stand beside the works of Virgil and Homer. Shakespeare is equally preoccupied with national identity. His history plays tell an epic story that examines how modern England came into being through the conflicts of the fifteenth-century Wars of the Roses which brought the Tudors to the throne. He is fascinated, too, by the related subject of politics and the exercise of power. With the collapse of medieval feudalism and the authority of local barons, the royal court in the Renaissance came to assume a new status as the centre of power and patronage. It was here that the destiny of a country was shaped. Courts, and how to succeed in them, consequently fascinated the Renaissance; and they fascinated Shakespeare and his audience.

But the dramatic gaze is not merely admiring; through a variety of devices, a critical perspective is brought to bear. The court may be paralleled by a very different world, revealing uncomfortable similarities (for example, Henry's court and the Boar's Head tavern, ruled over by Falstaff in *Henry IV*). Its hypocrisy may be bitterly denounced (for example, in the diatribes of the mad Lear) and its self-seeking ambition represented disturbingly in the figure of a Machiavellian villain (such as Edmund in *Lear*) or a malcontent (such as Iago in *Othello*). Shakespeare is fond of displacing the court to another context, the better to examine its assumptions and pretensions and to offer alternatives to the courtly life (for example, in the pastoral setting of the forest of Arden in *As You Like It* or

CHECK THE BOOK
Benedict Anderson's book on the rise of the nation and nationalism, *Imagined Communities* (revised ed., 1991), has been influential for its definition of the nation as 'an imagined political community' – imagined in part through cultural productions such as Shakespeare's history plays.

Prospero's island in *The Tempest*). Courtiers are frequently figures of fun whose unmanly sophistication ('neat and trimly dressed, / Fresh as a bridegroom ... perfumed like a milliner', says Hotspur of such a man in *1 Henry IV*, I.3.33–6) is contrasted with plain-speaking integrity: Oswald is set against Kent in *King Lear*.

When thinking of these matters, we should remember that stage plays were subject to censorship, and any criticism had therefore to be muted or oblique: direct criticism of the monarch or contemporary English court would not be tolerated. This has something to do with why Shakespeare's plays are always set either in the past, or abroad.

The nationalism of the English Renaissance was reinforced by Protestantism. Henry VIII had broken with Rome in the 1530s and in Shakespeare's time there was an independent Protestant state church. Because the Pope in Rome had excommunicated Queen Elizabeth as a heretic and relieved the English of their allegiance to the crown, there was deep suspicion of Roman Catholics as potential traitors. This was enforced by the attempted invasion of the Spanish Armada in 1588. This was a religiously inspired crusade to overthrow Elizabeth and restore England to Roman Catholic allegiance. Roman Catholicism was hence easily identified with hostility to England. Its association with disloyalty and treachery was then reinforced by the Gunpowder Plot of 1605, a Roman Catholic attempt to destroy the government of England.

Shakespeare's plays are remarkably free from direct religious sentiment, but their emphases are Protestant. Young women, for example, are destined for marriage, not for nunneries (precisely what Isabella appears to escape at the end of *Measure for Measure*); friars are dubious characters, full of schemes and deceptions, if with benign intentions, as in *Much Ado About Nothing* or *Romeo and Juliet*. (We should add that Puritans, extreme Protestants, are even less kindly treated than Roman Catholics: for example, Malvolio in *Twelfth Night*).

The central figures of the plays are frequently individuals beset by temptation, by the lure of evil – Angelo in *Measure for Measure*,

CHECK THE FILM
We can get a modern equivalent of the effect of this displacement from Christine Edzard's film of *As You Like It* (1992). Here, the court scenes are set in the luxurious headquarters of a bank or company; the woodland scenes amid a sort of 'cardboard city' of social outcasts and the vulnerable.

CHECK THE NET

Find out more about the Shakespearean theatre at **www.reading.ac.uk/globe**. This web site describes the historical researches undertaken in connection with the Globe theatre on London's Bankside, which was rebuilt in the late 1990s.

CONTEXT

The nineteenth-century tradition of using Oriental props and costumes when playing *Othello* has continued to the present day. A notable RSC production of the 1980s featured costumes that bore some resemblance to the garb worn by the Moorish ambassador to Elizabeth I, who was painted in 1600. This portrait has undoubtedly influenced the stage history of the play.

Othello, Lear, Macbeth – and not only in tragedies: Falstaff is described as 'that old white-bearded Satan' (*1 Henry IV*, II.4.454). We follow their inner struggles. Shakespeare's heroes have the preoccupation with self and the introspective tendencies encouraged by Protestantism: his tragic heroes are haunted by their consciences, seeking their true selves, agonising over what course of action to take as they follow what can often be understood as a kind of spiritual progress towards heaven or hell.

SHAKESPEARE'S THEATRE

The theatre for which the plays were written was one of the most remarkable innovations of the Renaissance. There had been no theatres or acting companies during the medieval period. Performed on carts and in open spaces at Christian festivals, plays had been almost exclusively religious. Such professional actors as there were wandered the country putting on a variety of entertainments in the yards of inns, on makeshift stages in market squares, or anywhere else suitable. They did not perform full-length plays, but mimes, juggling and comedy acts. Such actors were regarded by officialdom and polite society as little better than vagabonds and layabouts.

Just before Shakespeare went to London all this began to change. A number of young men who had been to the universities of Oxford and Cambridge came to London in the 1580s and began to write plays that made use of what they had learned about the classical drama of ancient Greece and Rome. Plays such as John Lyly's *Alexander and Campaspe* (1584), Christopher Marlowe's *Tamburlaine the Great* (about 1587) and Thomas Kyd's *The Spanish Tragedy* (1588–9) were unlike anything that had been written in English before. They were full-length plays on secular subjects, taking their plots from history and legend, adopting many of the devices of Classical drama, and offering a range of characterisation and situation hitherto unattempted in English drama. With the exception of Lyly's prose dramas, they were composed in the unrhymed iambic pentameters (blank verse), which the Earl of Surrey had introduced into English earlier in the sixteenth century. This was a freer and more expressive medium than the rhymed verse of medieval drama. It was the drama of these 'university wits' that Shakespeare challenged when he came to London. Greene was one of them, and we have heard how little he liked Shakespeare setting himself up as a dramatist.

The most significant change of all, however, was that these dramatists wrote for the professional theatre. In 1576 James Burbage built the first permanent theatre in England, in Shoreditch, just beyond London's northern boundary. It was called simply 'The Theatre'. Others soon followed. Thus, when Shakespeare came to London, there was a flourishing drama, theatres and companies of actors waiting for him, such as there had never been before in England. His company performed at James Burbage's Theatre until 1596, and used the Swan and Curtain until they moved into their own new theatre, the Globe, in 1599. It was burned down in 1613 when a cannon was fired during a performance of Shakespeare's *Henry VIII*.

With the completion in 1996 of Sam Wanamaker's project to construct in London a replica of the Globe, and with productions now running there, a version of Shakespeare's theatre can be experienced at first hand. It is very different to the usual modern experience of drama. The form of the Elizabethan theatre derived from the inn yards and animal baiting rings in which actors had been accustomed to perform in the past. They were circular wooden buildings with a paved courtyard in the middle open to the sky. A rectangular stage jutted out into the middle of this yard. Some of the audience stood in the yard (or 'pit') to watch the play. They were thus on three sides of the stage, close up to it and on a level with it. These 'groundlings' paid only a penny to get in, but for wealthier spectators there were seats in three covered tiers or galleries between the inner and outer walls of the building, extending round most of the auditorium and overlooking the pit and the stage. Such a theatre could hold about 3,000 spectators. The yards were about 80ft in diameter and the rectangular stage approximately 40ft by 30ft and 5ft 6in high. Shakespeare aptly called such a theatre a 'wooden O' in the prologue to *Henry V* (line 13).

The stage itself was partially covered by a roof or canopy, which projected from the wall at the rear of the stage and was supported

CHECK THE BOOK
The most authoritative book on what we know about the theatre of Shakespeare's time is Andrew Gurr's *The Shakespearean Stage* (1992).

CONTEXT
Whereas now we would conceptualise a visit to the theatre as going to *see* a play, the most common Elizabethan phrase was 'to go *hear* a play' (as in *The Taming of the Shrew*, Induction 2.130) – thus registering the different sensory priorities of the early modern theatre.

THE GLOBE THEATRE,

On the Bankside.

As it appeared in the reign of King James I.

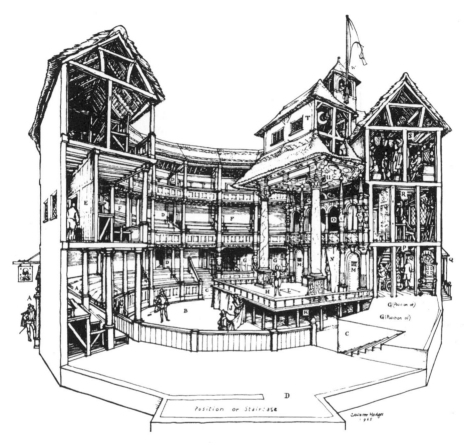

A CONJECTURAL RECONSTRUCTION OF THE INTERIOR OF THE GLOBE PLAYHOUSE

AA	Main entrance	N	Curtained 'place behind the stage'
B	The Yard	O	Gallery above the stage, used as required
CC	Entrances to lowest galleries		sometimes by musicians, sometimes by
D	Entrance to staircase and upper galleries		spectators, and often as part of the play
E	Corridor serving the different sections of the	P	Back-stage area (the tiring-house)
	middle gallery	Q	Tiring-house door
F	Middle gallery ('Twopenny Rooms')	R	Dressing-rooms
G	'Gentlemen's Rooms or Lords Rooms'	S	Wardrobe and storage
H	The stage	T	The hut housing the machine for lowering
J	The hanging being put up round the stage		enthroned gods, etc., to the stage
K	The 'Hell' under the stage	U	The 'Heavens'
L	The stage trap, leading down to the Hell	W	Hoisting the playhouse flag
MM	Stage doors		

by two posts at the front. This protected the stage and performers from inclement weather, and to it were secured winches and other machinery for stage effects. On either side at the back of the stage was a door. These led into the dressing room (or 'tiring house') and it was by means of these doors that actors entered and left the stage. Between these doors was a small recess or alcove which was curtained off. Such a 'discovery place' served, for example, for Juliet's bedroom when in Act IV Scene 4 of *Romeo and Juliet* the Nurse went to the back of the stage and drew the curtain to find Juliet apparently dead on her bed. Above the discovery place was a balcony, used for the famous balcony scenes of *Romeo and Juliet* (II.2 and III.5), or for the battlements of Richard's castle when he is confronted by Bolingbroke in *Richard II* (III.3). Actors (all parts in the Elizabethan theatre were taken by boys or men) had access to the area beneath the stage; from here, in the 'cellarage', would have come the voice of the ghost of Hamlet's father (*Hamlet*, II.1.150–82).

On these stages there was very little in the way of scenery or props – there was nowhere to store them (there were no wings in this theatre) nor any way to set them up (no tabs across the stage), and, anyway, productions had to be transportable for performance at court or at noble houses. The stage was bare, which is why characters often tell us where they are: there was nothing on the stage to indicate location. It is also why location is so rarely topographical, and much more often symbolic. It suggests a dramatic mood or situation, rather than a place: Lear's barren heath reflects his destitute state, as the storm his emotional turmoil.

None of the plays printed in Shakespeare's lifetime marks act or scene divisions. These have been introduced by later editors, but they should not mislead us into supposing that there was any break in Elizabethan performances such as might happen today while the curtains are closed and the set is changed. The staging of Elizabethan plays was continuous, with the many short 'scenes' of which Shakespeare's plays are often constructed following one after another in quick succession. We have to think of a more fluid, and much faster, production than we are generally used to: in the prologues to *Romeo and Juliet* (line 12) and *Henry VIII* (line 13)

Shakespeare speaks of the playing time as only two hours. It is because plays were staged continuously that exits and entrances are written in as part of the script: characters speak as they enter or leave the stage because otherwise there would be a silence while, in full view, they took up their positions. (This is also why dead bodies have to be carried off: they cannot get up and walk off.)

In 1608 Shakespeare's company, the King's Men, acquired the Blackfriars Theatre, a smaller, rectangular indoor theatre, holding about 700 people, with seats for all the members of the audience, facilities for elaborate stage effects and, because it was enclosed, artificial lighting. It has been suggested that the plays written for this 'private' theatre differed from those written for the Globe, since, as it cost more to go to a private theatre, the audience came from a higher social stratum and demanded the more elaborate and courtly entertainment which Shakespeare's romances provide. However, the King's Men continued to play at the Globe in the summer, using Blackfriars in the winter, and it is not certain that Shakespeare's last plays were written specifically for the Blackfriars theatre, or first performed there.

READING SHAKESPEARE

Shakespeare's plays were written for this stage, but there is also a sense in which they were written *by* the stage. The material and physical circumstances of their production in such theatres had a profound effect upon the nature of Elizabethan plays. Unless we bear this in mind, we are likely to find them very strange, for we will read with expectations shaped by our own familiarity with modern fiction and modern drama which is, by and large, realistic; it seeks to persuade us that what we are reading or watching is really happening. This is quite foreign to Shakespeare. If we try to read him like this, we shall find ourselves irritated by the improbabilities of his plot, confused by his chronology, puzzled by locations, frustrated by unanswered questions and dissatisfied by the motivation of the action. The absurd ease with which disguised persons pass through Shakespeare's plays is a case in point: why does no one recognise people they know so well? There is a great deal of psychological accuracy in Shakespeare's plays, but we are far from any attempt at realism.

CONTEXT

Shakespeare's acting company would not have had personal copies of the playscript. Instead, they would only have been given their own lines to learn.

 CHECK THE BOOK

Deborah Cartmell's *Interpreting Shakespeare on Screen* (2000) is recommended for its clear and interesting sense of the possibilities and the requirements of approaching Shakespeare through the cinema.

CONTEXT

The Romantic critic S. T. Coleridge argued that literature requires our 'willing suspension of disbelief': but it is not clear that the theatre of the Shakespearean period did require its audience to forget that they were in a theatre. Certainly, remarks calling attention to the theatrical setting are commonplace – in comedies such as *Twelfth Night* (III.4.125) and *As You Like It* II.7.139–43, and in tragedies including *Macbeth* (V.5.23–5) – making it more difficult to forget the theatricality of the stories depicted.

CONTEXT

The part of Othello was written for the famous leading actor Richard Burbage, who also played Hamlet.

The reason is that in Shakespeare's theatre it was impossible to pretend that the audience was not watching a contrived performance. In a modern theatre, the audience is encouraged to forget itself as it becomes absorbed by the action on stage. The worlds of the spectators and of the actors are sharply distinguished by the lighting: in the dark auditorium the audience is passive, silent, anonymous, receptive and attentive; on the lighted stage the actors are active, vocal, demonstrative and dramatic. (The distinction is, of course, still more marked in the cinema.) There is no communication between the two worlds: for the audience to speak would be interruptive; for the actors to address the audience would be to break the illusion of the play. In the Elizabethan theatre, this distinction did not exist, and for two reasons: first, performances took place in the open air and in daylight which illuminated everyone equally; secondly, the spectators were all around the stage (and wealthier spectators actually on it), and were dressed no differently from the actors, who wore contemporary dress. In such a theatre, spectators would be as aware of each other as of the actors; they could not lose their identity in a corporate group, nor could they ever forget that they were spectators at a performance. There was no chance that they could believe 'this is really happening'.

This, then, was communal theatre, not only in the sense that it was going on in the middle of a crowd but also in the sense that the crowd joined in. Elizabethan audiences had none of our deference: they did not keep quiet, nor arrive on time, nor remain for the whole performance. They joined in, interrupted, even getting on the stage. And plays were preceded and followed by jigs and clowning. It was all much more like our experience of a pantomime, and at a pantomime we are fully aware, and are meant to be aware, that we are watching games being played with reality. The conventions of pantomime revel in their own artificiality: the fishnet tights are to signal that the handsome prince is a woman, the Dame's monstrous false breasts signal that 'she' is a man.

Something very similar is the case with Elizabethan theatre: it utilised its very theatricality. Instead of trying to persuade spectators that they are not in a theatre watching a performance,

Elizabethan plays acknowledge the presence of the audience. It is addressed not only by prologues, epilogues and choruses, but also in soliloquies. There is no realistic reason why characters should suddenly explain themselves to empty rooms, but, of course, there is no empty room. The actor is surrounded by people. Soliloquies are not addressed to the world of the play; they are for the audience's benefit. And that audience's complicity is assumed: when a character like Prospero declares himself to be invisible, it is accepted that he is. Disguises are taken to be impenetrable, however improbable, and we are to accept impossibly contrived situations, such as barely hidden characters remaining undetected (indeed, on the Elizabethan stage there was nowhere at all they could hide).

These, then, are plays that are aware of themselves as dramas; in critical terminology, they are self-reflexive, commenting upon themselves as dramatic pieces and prompting the audience to think about the theatrical experience. They do this not only through their direct address to the audience but also through their fondness for the play-within-a-play (which reminds the audience that the encompassing play is also a play) and their constant use of images from, and allusions to, the theatre. They are fascinated by role-playing, by acting, appearance and reality. Things are rarely what they seem, either in comedy (for example, in *A Midsummer Night's Dream*) or tragedy (*Romeo and Juliet*). This offers one way to think about those disguises: they are thematic rather than realistic. Kent's disguise in *Lear* reveals his true, loyal self, while Edmund, who is not disguised, hides his true self. In *As You Like It*, Rosalind is more truly herself disguised as a man than when dressed as a woman.

The effect of all this is to confuse the distinction we would make between 'real life' and 'acting'. The case of Rosalind, for example, raises searching questions about gender roles, about how far it is 'natural' to be womanly or manly: how does the stage, on which a man can play a woman playing a man (and have a man fall in love with him/her), differ from life, in which we assume the roles we think appropriate to masculine and feminine behaviour? The same is true of political roles: when a Richard II or Lear is so aware of the regal part he is performing, of the trappings and rituals of kingship,

CONTEXT

The famous tragedian Edmund Kean (1787–1833) played both Othello and Iago. His innovation was to play Othello as a 'tawny Moor'. He claimed that the poet and writer Coleridge had suggested that this was Othello's racial origin.

CHECK THE NET

The 'Designing Shakespeare' database at PADS (**www.pads.ahds. ac.uk**) has an extensive collection of photographs from different productions available online.

CONTEXT

The poet Walter Raleigh wrote a poem on this image of life as theatre, which begins 'What is our life? A play of passion', in which 'our mothers' wombs the tiring houses be / When we are dressed for this short comedy'. There's a twist at the end of the short verse: 'only we die in earnest, that's no jest'.

their plays raise the uncomfortable possibility that the answer to the question of what constitutes a successful king is simply: a good actor. Indeed, human life generally is repeatedly rendered through the imagery of the stage, from Macbeth's 'Life's but a walking shadow, a poor player / That struts and frets his hour upon the stage / And then is heard no more' (V.5.23–5) to Prospero's paralleling of human life to a performance which, like the globe (both world and theatre!) will end (IV.I.146–58). When life is a fiction, like this play, or this play is a fiction like life, what is the difference? 'All the world's a stage...' (*As You Like It*, II.7.139).

World events	Shakespeare's life (*dates for plays are approximate*)	Literature and the arts
1492 Columbus sails to America		
		1513 Niccolò Machiavelli, *The Prince*
1534 Henry VIII breaks with Rome and declares himself head of the Church of England		
1556 Archbishop Cranmer burnt at the stake		
1558 Elizabeth I accedes to throne		
	1564 Born in Stratford-upon-Avon	
		1565 Giambattisa Cinzio Giraldi, *The Hecatommithi*
		1565–7 English translation, by Arthur Golding, of *Ovid's Metamorphosis*
1568 Mary Queen of Scots taken prisoner by Elizabeth I		
1570 Elizabeth I excommunicated by Pope Pius V		
1571 The Battle of Lepanto		
		1576 Erection of the first specially built public theatres in London – the Theatre and the Curtain
1577 Francis Drake sets out on round the world voyage		
		1581 Barnabe Rich, *Farewell to Military Profession*
1582 Outbreak of the Plague in London	**1582** Marries Anne Hathaway	
	1583 His daughter, Susanna, is born	
1584 Raleigh's sailors land in Virginia		**1584** French translation, by Gabriel Chappuys, of Cinzio's *The Hecatommithi*
	1585 His twins, Hamnet and Judith, are born	
	late 1580s–early 90s Probably writes *Henry VI* (*Parts I, II, III*) and *Richard III*	
1587 Execution of Mary Queen of Scots after implication in plot to murder Elizabeth I		**1587** Christopher Marlowe, *Tamburlaine the Great*
	c1585–92 Moves to London	
1588 The Spanish Armada defeated		
1589 Accession of Henri IV to French throne		**c1589** Kyd, *The Spanish Tragedy* (first revenge tragedy)

CHRONOLOGY

World events	Shakespeare's life (*dates for plays are approximate*)	Literature and the arts
		1590 Spenser, *The Faerie Queene*
1592 Plague in London closes theatres	**1592** Writes *The Comedy of Errors*	**1592** Marlowe, *Doctor Faustus*
	1593 Writes *Titus Andronicus, The Taming of the Shrew*	
	1594 onwards Writes exclusively for the Lord Chamberlain's Men. Writes *Two Gentlemen of Verona, Love's Labours Lost, Richard II*	
	1595 Writes *Romeo and Juliet, A Midsummer Night's Dream*	
1596 Drake perishes on expedition to West Indies	**1596** Hamnet dies; William granted coat of arms	
	1598 Writes *Much Ado About Nothing*	**1598** Christopher Marlowe, *Hero and Leander*
	1599 Buys share in the Globe Theatre; Writes *Julius Caesar, As You Like It, Twelfth Night*	**1599** Translation, by Sir Lewes Lewkenor, of Cardinal Contareno's *The Commonwealth and Government of Venice*
	1600 *The Merchant of Venice* printed	**1600** John Parry, *History and Description of Africa*
	1600–1 Writes *Hamlet, The Merry Wives of Windsor*	
	1601 Writes *Troilus and Cressida*	
	1602 Writes *All's Well That Ends Well*	
	1602–4 Probably writes ***Othello***	
1603 Death of Queen Elizabeth I; accession of James I	**1603 onwards** His company enjoys patronage of James I as The King's Men	**1603** Marston's *The Malcontent* first performed
	1604 *Othello* performed; Writes *Measure for Measure*	

World events	Shakespeare's life (*dates for plays are approximate*)	Literature and the arts
1605 Discovery of Guy Fawkes's plot to blow up the Houses of Parliament	**1605** First version of *King Lear*	**1605** Cervantes, *Don Quijote de la Mancha*
	1606 Writes *Macbeth*	
	1606-7 Probably writes *Antony and Cleopatra*	
	1607 Writes *Coriolanus, Timon of Athens*	**1607** Tourneur's *The Revenger's Tragedy* published
	1608 Writes *Pericles*. The King's Men acquire Blackfriars Theatre for winter performances	
1609 Galileo constructs first astronomical telescope	**1609** Becomes part-owner of the new Blackfriars Theatre	
1610 Henri IV of France assassinated William Harvey discovers circulation of blood Galileo observes Saturn for the first time		
	1611 *Cymbeline, The Winter's Tale* and *The Tempest* performed	**1611** King James's translation of the Bible
1612 Last burning of heretics in England	**1612** Shakespeare retires from London theatre and returns to Stratford	**1612** Webster, *The White Devil*
	1613 The Globe Theatre burns down	**1613** Webster, *Duchess of Malfi*
	1616 Dies	
1618 Raleigh executed for treason Thirty Years War begins in England		
		1622 Birth of French dramatist Molière
	1623 *The First Folio* published	

FURTHER READING

THE TEXT AND ITS SOURCES

E.A.J. Honigmann, ed., *Othello*, The Arden Shakespeare, Nelson, London, 1997
>This is the edition of the text used in the preparation of these Notes. It includes a helpful introduction to the play which covers sources, characters and themes as well as some extracts from a translation of Cinzio's source novella

Kenneth Muir, *The Sources of Shakespeare's Plays*, Methuen, London, 1977
>This includes a detailed discussion of the various sources Shakespeare might have used, with a particular focus on and analysis of Cinzio's tale

Norman Sanders, ed., *Othello*, The New Cambridge Shakespeare, Cambridge University Press, 1984
>This edition also includes a useful introduction to the play which includes a stage history and interesting coverage of Shakespeare's sources

P. Williams, 'The 1622 quarto and the First Folio text of Othello', *Shakespeare Survey 5*, 1952, pp. 16–24

CRITICISM

Contemporary criticism

Harold Bloom, ed., *Othello*, Modern Critical Interpretations, Roundhouse Publishing, London, 1987
>Includes an analysis of the themes and structure of the play, and critical views

John Russell Brown, *Shakespeare: The Tragedies*, Palgrave Macmillan, Basingstoke, 2001
>Includes a lengthy chapter on various aspects of *Othello*. Written in a style that makes it accessible to A Level students as well as undergraduates. Split into short sections for ease of use

John Drakakis, ed., *Shakespearean Tragedy*, Longman, New York, 1992
>In this collection of contemporary criticism there are a range of views of *Othello* from different critics: Marilyn French (a **feminist** reading), Stephen Greenblatt (a **new historicist** reading), Andre Green (a **psychoanalytic** reading, which explores the homosexuality in the text). These critics discuss race, sexuality and the political dimensions of the tragedy

Barbara Everett, ' "Spanish" Othello: The Making of Shakespeare's Moor', *Shakespeare Survey 35*, 1982, pp. 101–12
>See this for a discussion about how Shakespeare portrays race in *Othello*.

Andrew Hadfield, ed., *Routledge Literary Sourcebook for Othello*, Routledge, London, 2002
   A broad-ranging guide to critical responses and contexts

Lisa Jardine, *Still Harping on Daughters: Women and Drama in the Age of Shakespeare*, Harvester Press, Brighton, 1983
   Jardine writes very persuasively about the sexual politics of *Othello*

Mythili Kaul, *Othello: New Essays by Black Writers*, Howard University Press, Harvard, 1997

Ania Loomba, *Gender, Race, Renaissance Drama*, Manchester University Press, 1987
   Loomba devotes a chapter to *Othello*, which she explores in relation to modern Indian society and Indian students' experiences of studying Shakespeare. She explores the sexual and racial politics of *Othello* in detail and also comments on Elizabethan attitudes towards race and colour

Virginia Mason Vaughan, *Othello: A Contextual History*, Cambridge University Press, Cambridge, 1996
   Examines contemporary writings and explores them in relation to the play e.g. representations of Africans and blackamoors, other tales involving jealous husbands, plus a history of *Othello* in performance in England and the US from 1660–1980s

Claire McEachern, ed., *The Cambridge Companion to Shakespearen Tragedy*, Cambridge Companions to Literature, Cambridge University Press, Cambridge, 2003
   Covers 10 plays in 13 essays. Essays included on cultural and literary background, the origins of sub genres of Shakespeare's tragedies e.g. love, revenge and classical tragedy, critical and theatrical reception of the plays

Kenneth Muir, ed., *Shakespeare Survey: Vol. 21, Othello*, Cambridge University Press, Cambridge, 2002
   A yearbook of Shakespeare studies and productions that focuses entirely on *Othello*

Lois Potter, *Othello*, Shakespeare in Performance, Manchester University Press, Manchester, 2002
   Traces acting traditions and how they affected interpretations of the central roles in the play. Looks at various stage and screen versions of the play, with detailed examination of Paul Robeson's portrayal of Othello. Useful for students who are interested in ethnic and cultural approaches to studying Shakespeare

Nicholas Potter, ed., *'Othello' – A Reader's Guide to Essential Criticism*, Readers Guides to Essential Criticism, Palgrave Macmillan, Basingstoke, 2000
   Traces the critical history of the play from the earliest critics up to the present day. Also covers the historical context of the play, the most significant themes and recurring critical concerns

Leonard Tennenhouse, *Power on Display: The Politics of Shakespeare's Genres*, Methuen, London, 1986
> In the chapter 'The Theater of Punishment: Jacobean tragedy and the politics of misogyny' Tennenhouse explores the representation of the female body and female sexuality in Jacobean drama, making some interesting comments about *Othello*; he suggests that women are punished when they threaten the social order with their sexuality

Earlier critics

S. L. Bethell, 'The diabolic images in Othello', *Shakespeare Survey 5*, 1952, pp. 62–80

A. C. Bradley, *Shakespearean Tragedy*, Macmillan, London 1904, third edition by J.R. Brown, Macmillan, Basingstoke, 1992
> Bradley focuses on character and motivation; this text has been very influential this century

T. S. Eliot, 'Shakespeare and the Stoicism of Seneca', *Selected Essays*, 1932

Helen Gardner, 'The Noble Moor', *Proceedings of the British Academy*, XLI, 1956
> Gardner explores the heroism of Othello and the nature of his love for Desdemona. She suggests that the hero and his love are flawed

R. B. Heilman, *Magic in the Web: Action and Language in 'Othello'*, Kentucky University Press, Lexington, 1956
> Heilman discusses language, symbolism, theme and character in a detailed analysis of the play

G. K. Hunter, '"Othello" and Colour Prejudice', *Proceedings of the British Academy*, LIII, 1967, pp. 139–63
> This lecture sheds light on Elizabethan attitudes towards colour and race, also covering the portrayal of Othello and Iago

F. R. Leavis, 'Diabolical Intellect and the Noble Hero', *The Common Pursuit*, Chatto and Windus, London, 1962
> Leavis writes in response to Bradley's ideas about *Othello*. He argues that Othello is responsible for his own downfall because of his deficient character

J. I. M. Stewart, *Character and Motive in Shakespeare*, Longman, London, 1949, reissued, 1965

John Wain, ed., *Shakespeare: 'Othello'*, Casebook series, Macmillan, 1971
> This collection includes comments and essays by Rymer, Samuel Johnson, Coleridge, Bradley, Eliot, Leavis, G. Wilson-Knight and other critics, up to the 1960s

Robert H. West, 'The Christianness of *Othello*', *Shakespeare Quarterly 15*, 1964, pp. 333–43
West offers a reading of the play that refutes the claims of critics who suggest that Othello is damned because of his sins

G. Wilson-Knight, 'The Othello Music', *The Wheel of Fire*, Methuen, London, revised edition, 1959

Shakespeare's theatre

For anyone interested in the history of the Elizabethan playhouses, staging practices and acting companies the following book is invaluable:

Andrew Gurr, *The Shakespearean Stage*, Cambridge University Press, 1980

blank verse unrhymed iambic pentameter: a line of five iambs. One of the commonest English metres. The popularity of blank verse is due to its flexibility and relative closeness to spoken English. It allows a pleasant variation of full strong stresses per line, generally four or five, while conforming to the basic metrical pattern of five iambs

characterisation the way in which a writer creates characters so as to attract or repel our sympathy. Different kinds of literature have certain conventions of characterisation. In Jacobean drama there were many stock dramatic 'types' (see Machiavel) whose characteristics were familiar to the audience.

dramatic irony a feature of many plays: it occurs when the development of the plot allows the audience to possess more information about what is happening than some of the characters themselves have. Iago is the source of much of the dramatic irony in *Othello*, informing the audience of his intentions. Characters may also speak in a dramatically ironic way, saying something that points to events to come without understanding the significance of their words

feminist feminism is, broadly speaking, a political movement claiming political and economic equality of women with men. Feminist criticism and scholarship seek to explore or expose the masculine 'bias' in texts and challenge traditional ideas about them, constructing and then offering a feminine perspective on works of art. Since the late 1960s feminist theories about literature and language, and feminist interpretations of texts have multiplied enormously. Feminism has its roots in previous centuries; early texts championing women's rights include Mary Wollstonecraft's *A Vindication of the Rights of Women* (1792) and J. S. Mill's *The Subjection of Women* (1869)

figurative any form of expression or grammar which deviates from the plainest expression of meaning is designated a 'figure of speech'. Departures into more decorative language are further defined by a large number of terms. Metaphor is probably the figure of speech which most clearly characterises literary language: hence 'figurative language' can specifically refer to metaphorical language as well as to language abounding in other figures of speech

hegemony leadership, the state which rules others, or the dominance of one state over others

hubris the self-indulgent confidence that causes a tragic hero to ignore the decrees, laws and warnings of the gods, and therefore defy them to bring about his or her downfall

irony in speech, irony consists of saying one thing while you mean another (many of Iago's speeches to his victims include examples of irony of this kind). However, not all ironical statements in literature are as easily discerned or understood; the patterns of irony – of situation, character, structure and vocabulary – in *Othello* need careful unravelling. In certain cases the context will make clear the true meaning intended, but sometimes the writer will have to rely on the reader sharing values and knowledge in order for his or her meaning to be understood. Ironic literature characteristically presents a variety of possible points of view about its subject matter

lexis a term used in linguistics: the vocabulary of a language

Machiavel the Machiavel was a villainous stock character in Elizabethan and Jacobean drama, so called after the Florentine writer Niccolo Machiavelli (1469–1527), author of *The Prince* (written 1513), a book of political advice to rulers that recommended the need under certain circumstances to lie to the populace for their own good and to preserve power. Embellishment of this suggestion (which was only one small part of his analysis of political power and justice) made Machiavelli almost synonymous with the Devil in English literature. Machiavels are practised liars and cruel political opportunists, who delight in their own manipulative evil. The topic of dissembling and disguising one's true identity amount almost to an obsession in plays in the early seventeenth century. Iago is one of the most sophisticated Machiavellian villains in Jacobean drama

new historicist the new historicism refers to the work of a loose affiliation of critics who discuss literary works in terms of their historical contexts. In particular, they seek to study literature as part of a wider cultural history, exploring the relationship of literature to society

oxymoron a figure of speech in which contradictory terms are brought together in what is at first sight an impossible combination. There are a number of examples in *Othello* e.g. Cassio is said to be 'damn'd in a fair wife' (I.1.21), Iago speaks of 'honest knaves' (I.1.49) and also informs us 'I am not what I am' (I.1.65). It seems particularly appropriate that oxymoron is a feature of Iago's speech since he is a white devil

psychoanalytic criticism Freud developed the theory of psychoanalysis as a means of curing neuroses in his patients, but its concepts were expanded by him and his followers as a means of understanding human behaviour and culture generally. Literature and the creative process always figured largely in his accounts of the human mind, as both example and inspiration: he asserted that many of his ideas had been anticipated in great literary works, and the terms he devised for his concepts (such as the Oedipus complex), illustrate his reliance on literary models. Critics who adopt a psychoanalytical approach explore the psychological conflicts in texts, seeking to uncover the latent content and psychological realities that underlie the work of art; they are looking at symbolism and hidden meanings

vice, the a figure in morality plays of the fifteenth and sixteenth centuries who tempts humankind in a half-comic, half-unpleasant manner. Many critics argue that Iago is modelled on this stock character

Rebecca Warren teaches English. She is the author of York Notes Advanced on *King Lear*, *The Taming of the Shrew*, *Richard III*, *The Mayor of Casterbridge*, *Sylvia Plath's Selected Poems* and *The Glass Menagerie*.

NOTES

Maya Angelou
I Know Why the Caged Bird Sings

Jane Austen
Pride and Prejudice

Alan Ayckbourn
Absent Friends

Elizabeth Barrett Browning
Selected Poems

Robert Bolt
A Man for All Seasons

Harold Brighouse
Hobson's Choice

Charlotte Brontë
Jane Eyre

Emily Brontë
Wuthering Heights

Shelagh Delaney
A Taste of Honey

Charles Dickens
David Copperfield
Great Expectations
Hard Times
Oliver Twist

Roddy Doyle
Paddy Clarke Ha Ha Ha

George Eliot
Silas Marner
The Mill on the Floss

Anne Frank
The Diary of a Young Girl

William Golding
Lord of the Flies

Oliver Goldsmith
She Stoops to Conquer

Willis Hall
The Long and the Short and the Tall

Thomas Hardy
Far from the Madding Crowd
The Mayor of Casterbridge
Tess of the d'Urbervilles
The Withered Arm and other Wessex Tales

L.P. Hartley
The Go-Between

Seamus Heaney
Selected Poems

Susan Hill
I'm the King of the Castle

Barry Hines
A Kestrel for a Knave

Louise Lawrence
Children of the Dust

Harper Lee
To Kill a Mockingbird

Laurie Lee
Cider with Rosie

Arthur Miller
The Crucible
A View from the Bridge

Robert O'Brien
Z for Zachariah

Frank O'Connor
My Oedipus Complex and Other Stories

George Orwell
Animal Farm

J.B. Priestley
An Inspector Calls
When We Are Married

Willy Russell
Educating Rita
Our Day Out

J.D. Salinger
The Catcher in the Rye

William Shakespeare
Henry IV Part I
Henry V
Julius Caesar
Macbeth
The Merchant of Venice
A Midsummer Night's Dream
Much Ado About Nothing

Romeo and Juliet
The Tempest
Twelfth Night

George Bernard Shaw
Pygmalion

Mary Shelley
Frankenstein

R.C. Sherriff
Journey's End

Rukshana Smith
Salt on the snow

John Steinbeck
Of Mice and Men

Robert Louis Stevenson
Dr Jekyll and Mr Hyde

Jonathan Swift
Gulliver's Travels

Robert Swindells
Daz 4 Zoe

Mildred D. Taylor
Roll of Thunder, Hear My Cry

Mark Twain
Huckleberry Finn

James Watson
Talking in Whispers

Edith Wharton
Ethan Frome

William Wordsworth
Selected Poems

A Choice of Poets

Mystery Stories of the Nineteenth Century including The Signalman

Nineteenth Century Short Stories

Poetry of the First World War

Six Women Poets

For the AQA Anthology:
Duffy and Armitage & Pre-1914 Poetry

Heaney and Clarke & Pre-1914 Poetry

Poems from Different Cultures